ISBN 978-1-330-44614-0
PIBN 10063379

This book is a reproduction of an important historical work. Forgotten Books uses
state-of-the-art technology to digitally reconstruct the work, preserving the original format
whilst repairing imperfections present in the aged copy. In rare cases, an imperfection in
the original, such as a blemish or missing page, may be replicated in our edition. We do,
however, repair the vast majority of imperfections successfully; any imperfections that
remain are intentionally left to preserve the state of such historical works.

1 MONTH OF
FREE
READING

at

www.ForgottenBooks.com

By purchasing this book you are eligible for one month membership to ForgottenBooks.com, giving you unlimited access to our entire collection of over 1,000,000 titles via our web site and mobile apps.

To claim your free month visit:

www.forgottenbooks.com/free63379

English
Français
Deutsche
Italiano
Español
Português

www.forgottenbooks.com

Mythology Photography **Fiction**
Fishing Christianity **Art** Cooking
Essays Buddhism Freemasonry
Medicine **Biology** Music **Ancient**
Egypt Evolution Carpentry Physics
Dance Geology **Mathematics** Fitness
Shakespeare **Folklore** Yoga Marketing
Confidence Immortality Biographies
Poetry **Psychology** Witchcraft
Electronics Chemistry History **Law**
Accounting **Philosophy** Anthropology
Alchemy Drama Quantum Mechanics
Atheism Sexual Health **Ancient History**
Entrepreneurship Languages Sport
Paleontology Needlework Islam
Metaphysics Investment Archaeology
Parenting Statistics Criminology
Motivational

AN AMERICAN AT OXFORD

BY

JOHN CORBIN

AUTHOR OF "SCHOOLBOY LIFE IN ENGLAND"

WITH ILLUSTRATIONS

BOSTON AND NEW YORK
HOUGHTON, MIFFLIN AND COMPANY
The Riverside Press, Cambridge
1903

W

TO

A. F. C.

PREFACE

BY a curious coincidence, the day on which the last proof of this book was sent to the printer saw the publication of the will of the late Cecil Rhodes, providing that each of the United States is forever to be represented at Oxford by two carefully selected undergraduate students. That the plan will result in any speedy realization of the ideals of the great exponent of English power in the new worlds is perhaps not to be expected. For the future of American education, on the other hand, few things could be more fortunate. Native and independent as our national genius has always been, and seems likely to remain, it has always been highly assimilative. In the past, we have received much needed aliment from the German universities. For the present, the elements of which we have most need may best, as I think, be assimilated from England.

Whether or not Americans at Oxford become imbued with Mr. Rhodes's conceptions as to the destiny of the English peoples, they can scarcely

fail to observe that Oxford affords to its undergraduates a very sensibly ordered and invigorating
life, a very sensibly ordered and invigorating education. This, as I have endeavored to point out
in the following pages, our American universities
do not now afford, nor are they likely to afford it
until the social and the educational systems are
more perfectly organized than they have ever
been, or seem likely to be, under the dominance
of German ideals. If, however, the new Oxford-
trained Americans should ever become an important factor in our university life, the future is
bright with hope. We have assimilated, or are
assimilating, the best spirit of German education ;
and if we were to make a similar draft on the
best educational spirit in England, our universities
would become far superior as regards their organization and ideals, and probably also as regards
what they accomplish, to any in Europe. The purpose and result of an introduction of English
methods would of course not be to imitate foreign
custom, but to give fuller scope to our native character, so that if the American educational ideals
in the end approximate the English more closely
than they do at present, such a result would be
merely incidental to the fact that the two countries

have at bottom much the same social character and instincts. If Mr. Rhodes's dream is to be realized, it will probably be in some such tardy and round-about but admirably vital manner as this.

At a superficial glance the testator's intention seems to have been to send the students to Oxford directly from American schools. Such a course, it seems to me, could only work harm. Even if the educational and residential facilities afforded at Oxford were on the whole superior to those of American universities, which they are not, the difᴶ ference could not compensate the student for the loss of his American university course with all it means in forming lifelong friendships among his countrymen and in assimilating the national spirit. If, however, the Oxford scholarships were awarded to recent graduates of American universities, the greatest advantage might result. The student might then modify his native training so as to complete it and make it more effective. Now the wording of the testament requires only that the American scholars shall "commence residence as undergraduates." This they will be able to do whatever their previous training, and in fact this is what Americans at Oxford have always done in the past. The most valuable A. B. leaves the field of human knowledge far from exhausted; and the methods of instruction and of examining at Oxford are so different from anything we know that it has even proved worth while for the American to repeat at Oxford the same studies he took in America. The executors of the will should be most vigorously urged to select the scholars from the graduates of American universities.

The parts of this book that treat most intimately of Oxford life were written while in residence in Balliol College some six years ago. Most of the rest was written quite recently in London. Much of the matter in the following pages has appeared in "Harper's Weekly," "The Bachelor of Arts," "The Forum," and "The Atlantic Monthly." It has all been carefully revised and rearranged, and much new matter added. Each chapter has gained, as I hope, by being brought into its natural relation with the other chapters; and the ideas that have informed the whole are for the first time adequately stated.

CONTENTS

CONTENTS

LIST OF ILLUSTRATIONS

AN AMERICAN AT OXFORD

THE great German historian of the United States, H. E. Von Holst, declares [1] that, "in the sense attached to the word by Europeans, . . . there is in the United States as yet not a single university;" institutions like Johns Hopkins and Harvard he characterizes as "hybrids of college and university." In his survey of European usage, one suspects that Professor Von Holst failed to look beyond Germany. The so-called universities of England, for example, are mere aggregations of colleges; they have not even enough of the modern scientific spirit to qualify as hybrids, having consciously and persistently refused to adopt continental standards. The higher institutions of America belong historically to the English type; they have only recently imported the scientific spirit. To the great world of graduates and undergraduates they are colleges, and should as far as possible be kept so.

Yet there is reason enough for calling them

[1] *Educational Review*, vol. v. p. 113.

hybrids. In the teaching bodies of all of them the German, or so-called university, spirit is very strong, and is slowly possessing the more advanced of our recent graduates and undergraduates. Let us be duly grateful. The first result of this spirit is an extraordinary quickening and diffusion of the modern ideal of scholarship, a devotion to pure science amounting almost to a passion. As to the second result, we may or may not have cause to be grateful. Our most prominent educational leaders have striven consciously to make over our universities on the German plan. We are in the midst of a struggle between old and new forces, and at present the alien element has apparently the upper hand. The social ideal, which only a few years ago was virtually the same in England and America, has already been powerfully modified; and the concrete embodiment of the new scientific spirit, the so-called elective system, has transformed the peculiar educational institution of our Anglo-Saxon people.

We have gone so far forward that it is possible to gain an excellent perspective on what we are leaving behind. In the ensuing pages I propose to present as plainly as I may the English university of colleges. I shall not hesitate to give its social life all the prominence it has in fact, devoting much space even to athletic sports. The peculiarity of the English ideal of education is that it aims to develop the moral and social virtues, no less than the mental — to train up boys to be men among men. Only by understanding this is it possible to sympathize with the system of instruction, its peculiar excellences, and its almost incredible defects. In the end I hope we shall see more clearly what our colleges have inherited from the parent institutions, and shall be able to judge how far the system of collegiate education expresses the genius of English and American people.

At the present juncture of political forces in America this consideration has a special importance. The success with which we exert our influence upon distant peoples will depend upon what manner of young men we train up to carry it among them. If the graduates of German institutions are prepared to establish their civilization in the imperial colonies, the fact has not yet been shown. The colleges of England have manned the British Empire.

I

THE UNIVERSITY AND THE COLLEGE

I

THE UNIVERSITY OF COLLEGES

ONE of the familiar sights at Oxford is the American traveler who stops over on his way from Liverpool to London, and, wandering up among the walls of the twenty colleges from the Great Western Station, asks the first undergraduate he meets which building is the university. When an Oxford man is first asked this, he is pretty sure to answer that there is n't any university; but as the answer is taken as a rudeness, he soon finds it more agreeable to direct inquirers to one of the three or four single buildings, scattered hither and yon among the ubiquitous colleges, in which the few functions of the university are performed. A traveler from our middle West, where "universities" often consist of a single building, might easily set forth for London with the firm idea that the Ashmolean Museum or the Bodleian Library is Oxford University.

To the undergraduate the university is an abstract institution that at most examines him two or three times, "ploughs" him, or graduates him.

He becomes a member of it by being admitted into one of the colleges. To be sure, he matriculates also as a student of the university; but the ceremony is important mainly as a survival from the historic past, and is memorable to him perhaps because it takes place beneath the beautiful mediæval roof of the Divinity School; perhaps because he receives from the Vice-Chancellor a copy of the university statutes, written in mediæval Latin, which it is to be his chief delight to break. Except when he is in for " schools," as the examinations are called, the university fades beyond his horizon. If he says he is " reading " at Oxford, he has the city in mind. He is more likely to describe himself as " up at " Magdalen, Balliol, or elsewhere. This English idea that a university is a mere multiplication of colleges is so firmly fixed that the very word is defined as " a collection of institutions of learning at a common centre." In the daily life of the undergraduate, in his religious observances, and in regulating his studies, the college is supreme.

To an American the English college is not at first sight a wholly pleasing object. It has walls that one would take to be insurmountable if they were not crowned with shards of bottles mortared into the coping; and it has gates that seem capable of resisting a siege until one notices that they are reinforced by a *cheval-de-frise*, or a row of bent spikes like those that keep the bears in their dens at the Zoo. Professor Von Holst would certainly regard it as a hybrid between a mediæval cloister and a nursery; and one easily imagines him producing no end of evidence from its history and traditions to show that it is so. Like so many English institutions, its outward and visible signs belong to the manners of forgotten ages, even while it is charged with a vigorous and very modern life. A closer view of it, I hope, will show that in spite of the barnacles of the past that cling to it — and in some measure, too, because of them — it is the expression of a very high ideal of undergraduate convenience and freedom.

THE OXFORD FRESHMAN

WHEN a freshman comes up to his college, he is received at the mediæval gate by a very modern porter, who lifts boxes and bags from the hansom in a most obliging manner, and is presently shown to his cloistral chambers by a friendly and urbane butler or steward. To accommodate the newcomers in the more populous colleges, a measure is resorted to so revolutionary that it shocks all American ideas of academic propriety. Enough seniors — fourth and third year men — are turned out of college to make room for the freshmen. The assumption is that the upper classmen have had every opportunity to profit by the life of the college, and are prepared to flock by themselves in the town. Little communities of four or five fellows who have proved congenial live together in "diggings" — that is, in some townsman's house — hard by the college gate. This arrangement makes possible closer and more intimate relationship among them than would otherwise be likely; and after three years of the very free life within those sharded walls, a cloistered year outside is usually more than advisable, in view of the final examination. It cannot be said that they leave college without regret; but I never heard a word of complaint, and it is tacitly admitted that on the whole they profit by the arrangement.

The more substantial furnishings in the rooms are usually permanent, belonging to the college : each successive occupant is charged for interest on the investment and for depreciation by wear. Thus the furniture is far more comfortable than in an American college room and costs the occupant less. Bed and table linen, cutlery, and a few of the more personal furnishings the student brings himself. If one neglects to bring them, as I confess I did through ignorance, the deficiency is supplied by the scout, a dignitary in the employ of the college, who stands in somewhat more than the place of a servant and less than that of a parent to half a dozen fellows whose rooms are adjacent. The scout levies on the man above for sheets, on the man below for knives and forks, and on the man across the staircase for table linen. There is no call for shame on the one part or resentment on the other, for is not the scout the representative of the hospitality of the college? " When you have time, sir," he says kindly, " you will order your own linen and cutlery." How high a state of civilization is implied in this manner of receiving a freshman can be appreciated only by those who have arrived friendless at an American university.

The scout is in effect a porter, "goody," and eating-club waiter rolled into one. He has frequently a liberal dash of the don, which he has acquired by extended residence at the university; for among all the shifting generations of undergraduates, only he and the don are permanent. When he reaches middle age he wears a beard if he chooses, and then he is usually taken for a don by the casual visitor. There is no harm in this; the scout plays the part *con amore*, and his long breeding enables him to sustain it to a marvel. Yet for the most part the scout belongs with the world of undergraduates. He has his social clubs and his musical societies; he runs, plays cricket, and rows, and, finally, he meets the Cambridge scout in the inter-varsity matches. His pay the scout receives in part from the college, but mostly from the students, who give him two to four pounds a term each, according to his deserts. All broken bread, meat, and wine are his perquisites, and tradition allows him to "bag" a fair amount of tea, coffee, and sugar. Out of all this he makes a sumptuous living. I knew only one exception,

and that was when four out of six men on a certain
scout's staircase happened to be vegetarians, and
five teetotalers.   The poor fellow was in extremities
for meat and in desperation for drink.   There was
only one more pitiable sight in college, and that
was the sole student on the staircase who ate meat
and drank wine; the scout bagged food and drink
from him ceaselessly.   At the end of one term the
student left a half dozen bottles of sherry, which
he had merely tasted, in his sideboard; and when
he came back it was gone.   "Where's my sherry,
Betts?" he asked.   "Sherry, sir? you ain't got
no sherry."   "But I left six bottles; you had no
right to more than the one that was broken."   "Yes,
sir; but when I had taken that, sir, the 'arf dozen
was broke."   According to Oxford traditions the
student had no recourse; and be it set down to his
praise, he never blamed the scout.   He bemoaned
the fate that bound them together in suffering, and
vented his spleen on total abstinence and vegeta-
rianism.   It may be supposed that the scout's an-
tiquity and importance makes him a bad servant;
in the land of the free I fear that it would; but
at Oxford nothing could be more unlikely.   The
only mark that distinguishes the scout from any
other class of waiters is that his attentions to your
comfort are carried off with greater ease and

dignity. It may be true that he is president of the Oxford Society of College Servants — the Bones or the Hasty Pudding of the scouts; that he stroked the scouts' eight in the townie's bumping races, during the long vac, and afterward rowed against the scouts' eight from Cambridge; that he captained the scouts' cricket eleven; that in consequence he is a " double blue " and wears the Oxford 'varsity color on his hat with no less pride than any other "blue." Yet he is all the more bound, out of consideration for his own dignity, to show you every respect and attention.

After the scout, the hosts of the college are the dons. As soon as the freshman is settled in his rooms, or sometimes even before, his tutor meets him and arranges for a formal presentation to the dean and master. All three are apt to show their interest in a freshman by advising him as to trying for the athletic teams, joining the college clubs and societies, and in a word as to all the concerns of undergraduate life except his studies — these come later. If a man has any particular gift, athletic or otherwise, the tutor introduces him to the men he should know, or, when this is not feasible, gives a word to the upper classmen, who take the matter into their own hands. If a freshman has no especial gift, the tutor is quite as sure to say the proper word to the fellows who have most talent for drawing out newcomers.

In the first weeks of a freshman's residence he finds sundry pasteboards tucked beneath his door: the upper classman's call is never more than the formal dropping of a card. The freshman is expected to return these calls at once, and is debarred by a happy custom from leaving his card if he does not find his man. He goes again and again until he does find him. By direct introduction from the tutor or by this formality of calling, the freshman soon meets half a dozen upper classmen, generally second-year men, and in due time he receives little notes like this : —

DEAR SMITH, — Come to my rooms if you can to breakfast with Brown and me on Wednesday at 8.30.

> Yours sincerely,
> A. ROBINSON.

At table the freshman finds other freshmen whose interests are presumably similar to his own.

No one supposes for a moment that all this is done out of simple human kindness. The freshman breakfast is a conventional institution for gathering together the unlicked cubs, so that the local influences may take hold of them. The reputation of the college in general demands that it keep up a name for hospitality ; and in particular the clubs and athletic teams find it of advantage to get the run of all available new material. The freshman breakfast is nothing in the world but a variation of the " running ' that is given newcomers in those American colleges where fraternity life is strong, and might even be regarded as a more civilized form of the rushes and cane sprees and even hazings that used to serve with us to introduce newcomers to their seniors. Many second-year breakfasts are perfunctory enough; the host has a truly British air of saying that since for better or for worse he is destined to look upon your face and abide by your deeds, he is willing to make the best of it. If you prove a " bounder," you are soon enough dropped. " *I* shall soon be a second-year man," I once heard a freshman remark, " and then *I* can ask freshmen to breakfast, too, and cut them afterward." The point is that every fellow is thrown in the way of meeting the men of his year. If one is neglected in the end, he has no reason to feel that it is the fault of the college. As a result of this machinery for initiating newcomers, a man usually ceases to be a freshman after a single term (two months) of residence; and it is always assumed that he does.

16

III

A DAY IN AN OXFORD COLLEGE

WHEN a freshman is once established in college, his life falls into a pleasantly varied routine. The day is ushered in by the scout, who bustles into the bedroom, throws aside the curtain, pours out the bath, and shouts, "Half past seven, sir," in a tone that makes it impossible to forget that chapel — or if one chooses, roll-call — comes at eight. Unless one keeps his six chapels or "rollers" a week, he is promptly "hauled" before the dean, who perhaps "gates" him. To be gated is to be forbidden to pass the college gate after dark, and fined a shilling for each night of confinement. To an American all this brings recollections of the paternal roof, where tardiness at breakfast meant, perhaps, the loss of dessert, and bedtime an hour earlier. I remember once, when out of training, deliberately cutting chapel to see with what mien the good dean performed his nursery duties. His calm was unruffled, his dignity unsullied. I soon came to find that the rules about rising were bowed to and indeed respected

17

by all concerned, even while they were broken. They are distinctly more lax than those the fellows have been accustomed to in the public schools, and they are conceded to be fo. the best welfare of the college.

Breakfast comes soon after chapel, or roll-call. If a man has " kept a dirty roller," that is, has reported in pyjamas, ulster, and boots, and has turned in again, the scout puts the breakfast before the fire on a trestle built of shovel, poker, and tongs, where it remains edible until noon. If a man has a breakfast party on, the scout makes sure that he is stirring in season, and, hurrying through the other rooms on the staircase, is presently on hand for as long as he may be wanted. The usual Oxford breakfast is a single course, which not infrequently consists of some one of the excellent English pork products, with an egg or kidneys. There may be two courses, in which case the first is of the no less excellent fresh fish. There are no vegetables. The breakfast is ended with toast and jam or marmalade. When one has fellows in to breakfast, — and the Oxford custom of rooming alone instead of chumming makes such hospitality frequent, — his usual meal is increased by a course, say, of chicken. In any case it leads to a morning cigarette, for tobacco aids digestion, and helps fill the hour or so after meals which an Englishman gives to relaxation.

At ten o'clock the breakfast may be interrupted for a moment by the exit of some one bent on attending a lecture, though one apologizes for such an act as if it were scarcely good form. An appointment with one's tutor is a more legitimate excuse for leaving; but even this is always an occasion for an apology, in behalf of the tutor of course, for one is certainly not himself responsible. If a quorum is left, they manage to sit comfortably by the fire, smoking and chatting in spite of lectures and tutors, until by mutual consent they scatter to glance at the " Times " and the " Sportsman " in the common-room, or even to get in a bit of reading.

Luncheon often consists of bread and cheese and jam from the buttery, with perhaps a half pint of bitter beer; but it may, like the breakfast, come from the college kitchen. In any case it is very light, for almost immediately after it everybody scatters to field and track and river for the exercise that the English climate makes necessary and the sport that the English temperament demands.

By four o'clock every one is back in college tubbed and dressed for tea, which a man serves himself in his rooms to as many fellows as he has been able to gather in on field or river. If he is eager to hear of the games he has not been able to witness, he goes to the junior common-room or to his club, where he is sure to find a dozen or so of kindred spirits representing every sport of importance. In this way he hears the minutest details of the games of the day from the players themselves; and before nightfall — such is the influence of tea — those bits of gossip which in America are known chiefly among members of a team have ramified the college. Thus the function of the " bleachers " on an American field is performed with a vengeance by the easy-chairs before a common-room fire; and a man had better be kicked off the team by an American captain than have his shortcomings served up with common-room tea.

The two hours between tea and dinner may be, and usually are, spent in reading.

IV

DINNER IN HALL

AT seven o'clock the college bell rings, and in two minutes the fellows have thrown on their gowns and are seated at table, where the scouts are in readiness to serve them. As a rule a man may sit wherever he chooses; this is one of the admirable arrangements for breaking up such cliques as inevitably form in a college. But in point of fact a man usually ends by sitting in some certain quarter of the hall, where from day to day he finds much the same set of fellows. Thus all the advantages of friendly intercourse are attained without any real exclusiveness. This may seem a small point; but an hour a day becomes an item in four years, especially if it is the hour when men are most disposed to be companionable.

The English College hall is a miniature of Memorial Hall at Harvard, of which it is the prototype. It has the same sombrely beautiful roof, the same richness of stained glass. It has also the same memorable and impressive canvases, though the worthies they portray are likely to be the

21

princes and prelates of Holbein instead of the soldiers, merchants, and divines of Copley and Gilbert Stuart. The tables are of antique oak, with the shadow of centuries in its grain, and the college plate bears the names and date of the Restoration. To an American the mugs he drinks his beer from seem old enough, but the Englishman finds them aggressively new. They are not, however, without endearing associations, for the mugs that preceded them were last used to drink a health to King Charles, and were then stamped into coin to buy food and drink for his soldiers. The one or two colleges that, for Puritan principles or thrift, or both, refused to give up their old plate, are not overproud of showing it.

Across the end of the hall is a platform for high table, at which the dons assemble as soon as the undergraduates are well seated. On Sunday night they come out in full force, and from the time the first one enters until the last is seated, the undergraduates rattle and bang the tables, until it seems as if the glass must splinter. When, as often happens, a distinguished graduate comes up, — the Speaker of the Commons to Balliol, or the Prime Minister to Christ Church, — the enthusiasm has usually to be stopped by a gesture from the master or the dean.

THE HALL STAIRCASE, CHRIST CHURCH

DINNER IN HALL

The dons at high table, like the British peers, mingle judicial with legislative functions. All disputes about sconces are referred to them, and their decrees are absolute. A sconce is a penalty for a breach of good manners at table, and is an institution that can be traced far back into the Middle Ages. The offenses that are sconcible may be summarized as punning, swearing, talking shop, and coming to hall after high table is in session. Take, for instance, the case of a certain oarsman who found the dinner forms rather too rigid after his first day on sliding seats. By way of comforting himself, he remarked that the Lord giveth and the Lord taketh away. Who is to decide whether he is guilty of profanity? The master, of course, and his assembled court of dons. The remark and the attendant circumstances are written on the back of an order-slip by the senior scholar present, and a scout is dispatched with it. Imagine, then, the master presenting this question to the dons: Is it profanity to refer by means of a quotation from Scripture to the cuticle one loses in a college boat? Suppose the dons decree that it is. The culprit has the alternative of paying a shilling to the college library, or ordering a tun of bitter beer. If he decides for beer, a second alternative confronts him: he may drink it down in one uninterrupted draft, or he may kiss the cup and send it circling the table. If he tries to floor the sconce and fails, he has to order more beer for the table; but if he succeeds, the man who sconced him has to pay the shot and order a second tun for the table. I never knew but one man to down a sconce. He did it between soup and fish, and for the rest of the evening was as drunk as ever was the Restoration lord who presented the silver tankard to the college.

After hall the dons go to the senior common-room for the sweet and port. At Trinity they have one room for the sweet and another for port. The students, meanwhile, in certain of the colleges, may go for dessert to the college store; that is to say, to a room beneath the hall, where the fancy groceries of the college stock are displayed for sale. There are oranges from Florida and Tangiers, dainty maiden blush apples from New England, figs and dates from the Levant, prunes and prunelles from Italy, candied apricots from France, and the superb English hothouse grapes, more luscious than Silenus ever crushed against his palate. There are sweets, cigarettes, and cigars. All are spread upon the tables like a Venetian painting of abundance; but at either end of the room stand two Oxford scouts, with account-books in their hands.

A fellow takes a Tangerine and, with a tap-room gesture, tilts to the scout as if to say, " Here's looking toward you, landlord ; " or, " I drink to your bonny blue eyes." But he is not confronted by a publican or barmaid ; only a grave underling of the college bursar, who silently records " Brown, orange, 2d.," and looks up to catch the next item. Two other fellows are flipping for cigars, and the second scout is gravely watching their faces to see which way the coin has fallen, recording the outcome without a sign. Some one asks, " How much are chocolate creams, Higgins ? " " Three ha'pence for four, sir," is the answer, and the student urges three neighbors to share his penny-'orth. The scout records, " Jones, c. c. $1\frac{1}{2}$d."

The minuteness of this bookkeeping is characteristic. The weekly battels (bills) always bear a charge of twopence for " salt, etc. ; " and once, when I had not ordered anything during an entire day, there was an unspecified charge of a penny in the breakfast column. I asked the butler what it meant. He looked at me horrified. " Why, sir, that is to keep your name on the books." No penny, I suppose, ever filled an office of greater responsibility, and I still can shudder at so narrow an escape. I asked if such elaborate bookkeeping was not very expensive. In America, I said, we should lump the charges **and** devote the saving to hiring a better chef. He explained that it had always been so managed; that the chef was thought very good, **sir**; and that by itemizing charges the young gentlemen who wished were enabled to live more cheaply. Obviously, when it costs a penny merely to keep your name on the books, there is need to economize.

After a quarter of an hour in the store the fellows drop off by twos and threes to read, or to take coffee in some one's room. With the coffee a glass of port is usually taken. Almost **all** the fellows have spirits and wines, which are sold by the college as freely as any other commodity. If a man wishes a cup served in his room, he has only to say so to his scout. If one waits long enough in the store, he is almost certain to be asked to coffee and wine. The would-be host circulates the room tapping the elect on the shoulder and speaking a quiet word, as they select Bones men at Yale. If half a dozen men are left in the store uninvited, one of them is apt to rise to the occasion and invite the lot. It scarcely matters how unpopular a fellow may be. The willingness to loaf is the touch of nature that makes all men kin.

After coffee more men fall off to their books; but the faithful are likely to spend the evening talking or playing cards — bridge, loo, napp, and whist, with the German importation of skat and the American importation of poker. In one college I knew, there was a nomadic roulette wheel that wandered from room to room pursued by the shadow of the dean, but seldom failed of an evening to gather its flock about it.

V

EVENING

IN the evening, when the season permits, the fellows sit out of doors after dinner, smoking and playing bowls. There is no place in which the spring comes more sweetly than in an Oxford garden. The high walls are at once a trap for the first warm rays of the sun and a barrier against the winds of March. The daffodils and crocuses spring up with joy as the gardener bids; and the apple and cherry trees coddle against the warm north walls, spreading out their early buds gratefully to the mild English sun. For long, quiet hours after dinner they flaunt their beauty to the fellows smoking, and breathe their sweetness to the fellows playing bowls. "No man," exclaims the American visitor, "could live four years in these gardens of delight and not be made gentler and nobler!" Perhaps! though not altogether in the way the visitor imagines. When the flush of summer is on, the loiterers loll on the lawn full length; and as they watch the insects crawl among the grass they make bets on them, just as the gravest and most reverend seniors have been known to do in America.

In the windows overlooking the quadrangle are boxes of brilliant flowers, above which the smoke of a pipe comes curling out. At Harvard some fellows have geraniums in their windows, but only the very rich; and when they began the custom an ancient graduate wrote one of those communications to the "Crimson," saying that if men put unmanly boxes of flowers in the window, how can they expect to beat Yale? Flower boxes, no sand. At Oxford they manage things so that anybody may have flower boxes; and their associations are by no means unmanly. This is the way they do it. In the early summer a gardener's wagon from the country draws up by the college gate, and the driver cries, "Flowers! Flowers for a pair of old bags, sir." *Bags* is of course the fitting term for English trousers — which don't fit; and I should like to inform that ancient graduate that the window boxes of Oxford suggest the very badge of manhood.

As long as the English twilight lingers, the men will sit and talk and sing to the mandolin; and I have heard of fellows sitting and talking all night, not turning in until the porter appeared to take their names at roll-call. On the eve of May day it is quite the custom to sit out, for at dawn one may go·to see the pretty ceremony of heralding the May on Magdalen Tower. The Magdalen choir boys — the sweetest songsters in all Oxford — mount to the top of that most beautiful of Gothic towers, and, standing among the pinnacles, — pinnacles afire with the spirituality of the Middle Ages, that warms all the senses with purity and beauty, — those boys, I say, on that tower and among those pinnacles, open their mouths and sing a Latin song to greet the May. Meantime, the fellows who have come out to listen in the street below make catcalls and blow fish horns. The song above is the survival of a Romish, perhaps a Druidical, custom; the racket below is the survival of a Puritan protest. That is Oxford in symbol! Its dignity and mellowness are not so much a matter of flowering gardens and crumbling walls as of the traditions of the centuries in which the whole life of the place has deep sources; and the noblest of its institutions are fringed with survivals that run riot in the grotesque.

If a man intends to spend the evening out of college, he has to make a dash before nine o'clock; for love or for money the porter may not let an inmate out after nine. One man I knew was able to escape by guile. He had a brother in Trinity

MAGDALEN TOWER FROM THE BRIDGE

whom he very much resembled, and whenever he wanted to go out, he would tilt his mortarboard forward, wrap his gown high about his neck, as it is usually worn of an evening, and bidding the porter a polite good-night, say, " Charge me to my brother, Hancock, if you please." The charge is the inconsiderable sum of one penny, and is the penalty of having a late guest. Having profited by my experience with the similar charge for keeping my name on the college books, I never asked its why and wherefore. Both are no doubt survivals of some mediæval custom, the authority of which no college employee — or don, for the matter of that — would question. Such matters interest the Oxford man quite as little as the question how he comes by a tonsil or a vermiform appendix. They are there, and he makes the best of them.

If a fellow leaves college for an evening, it is for a foregathering at some other college, or to go to the theatre. As a rule he wears a cloth cap. A " billycock " or " bowler," as the pot hat is called, is as thoroughly frowned on now in English colleges as it was with us a dozen years ago. As for the mortarboard and gown, undergraduate opinion rather requires that they be left behind. This is largely, no doubt, because they are required by law to be worn. So far as the undergraduates are concerned, every operative statute of the university, with the exception of those relating to matriculation and graduation, refers to conduct in the streets after nightfall, and almost without exception they are honored in the breach. This is out of disregard for the Vice-Chancellor of the university, who is familiarly called the Vice, because he serves as a warning to others for the practice of virtue. The Vice makes his power felt in characteristically dark and tortuous ways. His factors are two proctors, college dons in daytime, but skulkers after nightfall, each of whom has his bulldogs, that is, scouts employed literally to spy upon the students. If these catch you without cap or gown, they cause you to be proctorized or "progged," as it is called, which involves a matter of five shillings or so. As a rule there is little danger of progging, but my first term fell in evil days. For some reason or other the chest of the university showed a deficit of sundry pounds, shillings, and pence; and as it had long ceased to need or receive regular bequests, — the finance of the institution being in the hands of the colleges, — a crisis was at hand. A more serious problem had doubtless never arisen since the great question was solved of keeping undergraduates' names on the books. The expedient of the Vice-Chancellor was

to summon the proctors, and bid them charge their
bulldogs to prog all freshmen caught at night without cap and gown. The deficit in the university
chest was made up at five shillings a head.

One of the Vice-Chancellor's rules is that no
undergraduate shall enter an Oxford "pub." Now
the only restaurant in town, Queen's, is run in
conjunction with a pub, and was once the favorite
resort of all who were bent on breaking the monotony of an English Sunday. The Vice-Chancellor resolved to destroy this den of Sabbath-
breaking, and the undergraduates resolved no less
firmly to defend their stronghold. The result
was a hand-to-hand fight with the bulldogs, which
ended so triumphantly for the undergraduates that
a dozen or more of them were sent down. In the
articles of the peace that followed, it was stipulated, I was told, that so long as the restaurant
was closed Sunday afternoons and nights, it should
never suffer from the visit of proctor or bulldog.
As a result, Queen's is a great scene of undergraduate foregatherings. The dinners are good
enough and reasonably cheap; and as most excellent champagne is to be had at twelve shillings the
bottle, the diners are not unlikely to get back to
college a trifle buffy, in the Oxford phrase.

By an interesting survival of mediæval custom,

the Vice-Chancellor has supreme power over the morals of the town, and any citizen who transgresses his laws is visited with summary punishment. For a tradesman or publican to assist in breaking university rules means outlawry and ruin, and for certain offenses a citizen may be punished by imprisonment. Over the Oxford theatre the Vice-Chancellor's power is absolute. In my time he was much more solicitous that the undergraduate be kept from knowledge of the omnipresent woman with a past than that dramatic art should flourish, and forbade the town to more than one excellent play of the modern school of comedy that had been seen and discussed in London by the younger sisters of the undergraduates. The woman with a present is virtually absent.

Time was when no Oxford play was quite successful unless the undergraduates assisted at its first night, though in a way very different from that which the term denotes in France. The assistance was of the kind so generously rendered in New York and Boston on the evening of an athletic contest. Even to-day, just for tradition's sake, the undergraduates sometimes make a row. A lot of B. N. C. men, as the clanny sons of Brazenose College call themselves, may insist that an opera stop while the troupe listen to one of their own excellent vocal performances ; and I once saw a great sprinter, not unknown to Yale men, rise from his seat, face the audience, and, pointing with his thumb over his shoulder at the soubrette, announce impressively, " Do you know, I rather *like* that girl ! " The show is usually over just before eleven, and then occurs an amusing, if unseemly, scramble to get back to college before the hour strikes. A man who stays out after ten is fined threepence ; after eleven the fine is sixpence. When all is said, why should n't one sprint for threepence ?

If you stay out of college after midnight, the dean makes a star chamber offense of it, fines you a " quid " or two, and like as not sends you down. This sounds a trifle worse than it is ; for if you must be away, your absence can usually be arranged for. If you find yourself in the streets after twelve, you may rap on some friend's bedroom window and tell him of your plight through the iron grating. He will then spend the first half of the night in your bed and wash his hands in your bowl. With such evidence as this to support him, the scout is not apt, if sufficiently retained, to report a suspected absence. I have even known fellows to make their arrangements in advance and spend the night in town ; but the ruse has its dangers, and the penalty is to be sent down for good and all.

It is owing to such regulations as these that life in the English college has the name of being cloistral. Just how cloistral it is in spirit no one can know who has not taken part in a rag in the quad; and this is impossible to an outsider, for at midnight all visitors are required to leave, under a heavy penalty to their host.

VI

THE MIND OF THE COLLEGE

ANY jubilation is a rag; but the most interesting kind, though perhaps the least frequent, takes the direction of what we call hazing. It is seldom, however, as hazing has come to be with us, a wanton outbreak. It is a deliberate expression of public opinion, and is carried on sedately by the leading men of the college. The more I saw of it, the more deeply I came to respect it as an institution.

In its simplest if rarest form it merely consists in smashing up a man's room. The only affair of this kind which I saw took place in the owner's absence; and when I animadverted on the fact, I was assured that it would have turned out much worse for the man's feelings if he had been present. He was a strapping big Rugbeian, who had come up with a "reputter," or reputation, as a football player, and had insisted on trying first off for the 'varsity fifteen. He had promptly been given the hoof for being slow and lazy, and when he condescended to try for the college fifteen, his services were speedily dispensed with for the same reason. As he still carried his head high, it was necessary to bring his shortcomings home to him in an unmistakable manner. Brutal as I thought the proceeding, and shameful to grown men, it did him good. He became a hard-working and lowly minded athlete, and prospered. I am not prepared to say that the effect in this particular instance did not justify the means.

A series of judicial raggings was much more edifying. Having pulled their culprit out of bed after midnight, the upper classmen set him upon his window-seat in pyjamas, and with great solemnity appointed a judge, a counsel for the prosecution, and a counsel for the defense. Of the charges against him only one or two struck home, and even these were so mingled with the nonsense of the proceedings that their sting was more or less blunted. The man had been given over to his books to the neglect of his personal appearance. It was charged that in pretending to know his subjunctives he was ministering to the vanity of the dean, who had written a Latin grammar, and that by displaying familiarity with Hegel he was bootlicking the master, who was a recently imported Scotch philosopher. Then the vital question was raised as to the culprit's personal habits. Heaven defend him now from his legal defender! It was urged that as he was a student of Literæ Humaniores, he might be excused from an acquaintance with the scientific commodity known as H_2O : one might ignore anything, in fact, if only one were interested in Literæ Humaniores. By such means as this the face of the college is kept bright and shining.

Here is a round robin, addressed to the best of fellows, a member of the 'varsity shooting team and golf team. He was a Scotchman by birth and by profession, and even his schoolboy days at Eton had not divested him of a Highland gait.

" Whereas, Thomas Rankeillor, Gent, of the University of Oxford, has, by means of his large feet, uncouth gait, and his unwieldy brogues, wantouly and with malice destroyed, mutilated, and otherwise injured the putting greens, tees, and golf course generally, the property of the Oxford University Golf Club, whereof he is a member, and

" Whereas, 2, The said Thomas Rankeillor, etc., has by these large feet, uncouth gait, and unwieldy brogues aforesaid, raised embankments, groins, and other bunkers, hazards, and impediments, formed unnecessary roads, farm roads, bridle paths, and other roads, on the putting greens, tees, and golf course generally, aforesaid; excavated sundry and diverse reservoirs, tanks, ponds, conduits, sewers, channels, and other runnels, needlessly irrigating the putting greens, tees, and golf course generally aforesaid, and

" Whereas, 3, The said Thomas Rankeillor, etc., has by those large feet, uncouth gait, and unwieldy brogues aforesaid, caused landslips, thus demolishing all natural hills, bunkers, and other excrescences, and all artificial hillocks, mounds, hedges, and other hazards,

" Hereby we, the circumsigned, do request, petition, and otherwise entreat the aforesaid

" THOMAS RANKEILLOR, GENT, OF THE UNIVERSITY OF OXFORD, to alter, transform, and otherwise modify his uncouth gait, carriage, and general mode of progression; to buy, purchase, or otherwise acquire boots, shoes, and all other understandings of reasonable size, weight, and material; and finally that he do cease from this time forward to wear, use, or in any way carry the aforesaid brogues.

" Given forth this the 17th day of March, 1896."

At times rougher means are employed. At Brazenose there happened to be two men by the same name, let us say, of Gaylor, one of whom had made himself agreeable to the college, while the other had decidedly not. One midnight a party of roisterers hauled the unpopular Gaylor out of his study, pulled off his bags, and dragged him by the heels a lap or two about the quad. This form of discipline has since been practiced in other colleges, and is called debagging. The popular Gaylor was ever afterward distinguished by the name of Asher, because, according to the Book of Judges, Asher abode in his breaches.

Not dissimilar correctives may be employed, in extreme need, against those mightiest in authority. A favorite device is to screw the oak of an objectionable don. Mr. Andrew Lang, himself formerly a don at Merton, reports a conversation — can it have been a personal experience? — between a don standing inside a newly screwed oak and his scout, who was tendering sympathy from the staircase. "What *am* I to do?" cried the don. "Mr. Muff, sir," suggested the scout, "when 'e 's screwed up, sir, 'e sends for the blacksmith." At Christ Church, "The House," as it is familiarly called, much more direct and personal methods have been employed. Not many years ago a censor (whose office is that of the dean at other colleges) stirred up unusual ill-will among his wards. They pulled him from his bed, dragged him into Tom Quad, — Wolsey's Quad, — and threw him bodily among the venerable carp of the Mercury Pond. Then they gathered about in a circle, and, when he raised his head above the surface, thrust him under with their walking-sticks. Something like forty of them were sent down for this, and the censor went traveling for his health.

The memory of this episode was still green when the Duke of Marlborough gave a coming of age ball at Blenheim Palace, and invited over literally hundreds of his Oxford friends. In other colleges the undergraduates were permitted to leave Oxford for the night, but at the House the censor stipulated that they be within the gates, as usual, by midnight. This would have meant a break-neck drive of eight miles after about fifteen minutes at the ball, and was far more exasperating to the young Britons than a straightforward refusal. That evening the dons sported their oaks, and carefully bolted themselves within. The night passed in so deep a silence that, for all they knew, the ghost of Wolsey might have been stalking in his cherished quadrangle, the glory of building which the Eighth Henry so unfeelingly appropriated. As morning dawned, the common-room gossips will tell you, the dons crawled furtively out of bed, and shot their bolts to find whether they had need of the blacksmith. Not a screw had been driven. The morning showed why

On the stately walls of Tom Quad was painted
"Damn the Dons!" and again in capital letters,
"Damn the Dons!" and a third time, in larger
capitals, "Damn the Dons!" There were other
inscriptions, less fit to relate; and stretching along
one whole side of the quad, in huge characters, the
finely antithetical sentence: "God bless the Duke
of Marlborough." The doors of the dean's residence were smeared with red paint; and against a
marble statue of the late Dean Liddell, the Greek
lexicographer, a bottle of green ink had been
smashed. Two hundred workmen, summoned
from a neighboring building, labored two days
with rice-root brushes and fuller's earth, but with
so little effect that certain of the stones had to be
replaced in the walls, and endless scrubbings
failed to overcome the affinity between the ink and
the literary Liddell. The marble statue has been
replaced by one of plaster.

Compared with the usual Oxford rag, the up-
setting of Professor Silliman's statue in the Yale
campus by means of a lasso dwindles into insig-
nificance, and the painting of 'varsity stockings on
John Harvard, which so scandalized the undergraduates that they repaired the damage by volun-
tary subscriptions, might be regarded as an act of
filial piety.

The more I learned of Oxford motives, the less anxious I was to censure the system of ragging. In an article I wrote after only a few months' stay, I spoke of it as boyish and undignified; and most Americans, I feel sure, would likewise hold up the hand of public horror. Yet I cannot be wholly thankful that we are not as they. To the undergraduates, ragging is a survival of the excellently efficient system of discipline in the public schools, where the older boys have charge of the manners and morals of the younger; and historically, like public school discipline, it is an inheritance from the prehistoric past. In the Middle Ages it was apparently the custom to hold the victim's nose literally to the grindstone. In the schools, to be sure, the Sixth Form take their duties with great sobriety of conscience — which is not altogether the case in college; but the difference of spirit is perhaps justifiable. For a properly authorized committee of big schoolboys to chastise a youngster who has transgressed is not unnatural, and the system that provides for it has proved successful for five centuries; but for men to adopt the same attitude towards a fellow only a year or two their junior would be preposterous. Horseplay is a necessary part of the game. The end in both is the same: it is to bring each individual under the influence of the traditions and standards of the institution of which he has elected to be a part. Just as the system of breakfasting freshmen is by no means as altruistic as it at first appears, the practice of ragging is by no means as brutal. It is as if the college said: We have admitted you and welcomed you, opening up the way to every avenue of enjoyment and profit, and it is for our common good, sir, that you be told of your shortcomings. The most diligent and distinguished scholar is not unlikely to be most in need of a pointed lesson in personal decorum; and the man who was not Asher may be thankful all his life for the bad quarter of an hour that taught him the difference between those who do and those who do not abide in their breaches.

With regard to the dons, a similar case might be made. Any one who assumes an authority over grown men that is so nearly absolute should be held to strict honesty and justice of dealing. So far as I could learn, the Christ Church dons who were so severely dealt with were both unjust and insincere, and I came to sympathize in some measure with the undergraduates at the House, who were half humorously inclined to regard the forty outcasts as martyrs.

This is not to argue that all American hazing

is justifiable. In many cases, especially of late years, it has been as silly and brutal as the most puritanical moralists have declared. To steal the Louisburg Cross from above the door of the Harvard Library was vandalism if you wish — it was certainly a very stupid proceeding; and to celebrate a really notable athletic victory by mutilating the pedestal of the statue of John Harvard was not only stupid, but unworthy of a true sportsman. How much better to make an end with painting 'varsity stockings on the dear old boy's bronze legs, and leave the goody to wash them off next day. What I wish to point out is that where there is vigorous public spirit, it may be more efficiently expressed by hazing than by a very nor'-easter of Puritan morality.

A tradition of the late master of Balliol, Jowett, the great humanist, would seem to show that he held some such opinion. It was his custom in his declining years to walk after breakfast in the garden quad, and whenever there were evidences of a rag, even to the extent of broken windows, he would say cheerily to his *fidus Achates*, " Ah, Hardie, the mind of the college is still vigorous; it has been expressing itself." The best possible justification of the cloistral restrictions of English college life is the facility with which the mind of the college expresses itself. It is by no means fantastic to hint that the decline of well-considered hazing in American colleges has come step by step with the breaking up of the bonds of hospitality and comradeship that used to make them well-organized social communities.

I have not come to this philosophy without deep experience. On one occasion after Hall, I was flown with such insolence against college restrictions that the *cheval-de-frise* above the back gate seemed an affront to a freeborn American. Though the porter's gate was still open, it was imperatively necessary to scale that roller of iron spikes. I was no sooner astride of it than a mob of townspeople gathered without, and among them a palsied beggar, who bellowed out that he would hextricate me for 'arf a crown, sir. I have seldom been in a less gratifying position; and when I had clambered back into college, I ruefully recalled the explanation my tutor had given me of the iron spikes and bottle shards, — an explanation that at the time had shaken my sides with laughter at British absurdity. My tutor had said that if the fellows were allowed to rag each other in the open streets and smash the townspeople's windows, the matter would be sure to get into the papers and set the uninitiated parent against the universities. In effect, the iron spikes and the stumps of bottles are admirable, not so much because they keep the undergraduate in, as because they keep the public out; and since the public includes all people who wish to hextricate you for 'arf a crown, sir, my mind was in a way to be reduced to that British state of illogic in which I regarded only the effect.

As a last resort I carefully sounded the undergraduates as to whether they would find use for greater liberty. They were not only content with their lot, but would, I found, resent any loosening of the restrictions. To give them the liberty of London at night or even of Oxford, they argued, would tend to break up the college as a social organization and thus to weaken it athletically; for at Oxford they understand what we sometimes do not, that a successful cultivation of sports goes hand in hand with good comradeship and mutual loyalty.

The only question remaining was of the actual moral results of the semi-cloistral life. Such outbreaks of public opinion as I have described are at the worst exceptional; they are the last resort of outraged patience. The affair at Christ Church is unexampled in modern times. Many a man of the better sort goes through his four years at the university without either experiencing or witnessing undergraduate violence. As for drinking, in spite of the fact that wine and spirits are sold to undergraduates by the college at any and all times and in any and all quantities, there seemed to be less excessive indulgence than, for instance, at Harvard or at Yale. And the fact that what there was took place for the most part within the college walls was in many respects most fortunate. When fellows are turned loose for their jubilations amid the vices of a city, as is usually the case with us, the consequences to their general morality are sometimes the most hideous. In an English college the men to whom immorality seems inevitable — and such are to be found in all communities — have recourse to London. But as their expeditions take place in daylight and cold blood, and are, except at great risk, cut short when the last evening train leaves Paddington shortly after dinner, it is not possible to carry them off with that dazzling air of the man of the world that in America lures so many silly freshmen into dissipations for which they have no natural inclination. This little liberty is apparently of great value. The cloistral vice, which seems inevitable in the English public schools, is robbed of any shadow of palliation. A fellow who continues it is thought puerile, if nothing worse. When it exists, it is more likely to be the result of the intimate study of the ancient classics, and is then even more looked down upon by the robust Briton as effeminate or decadent. The subject, usually difficult or impossible to investigate, happened to be on the surface at the time of my residence because of the sensational trial of an Oxford graduate in London. I was satisfied that the general body of undergraduates was quite free of contamination. On the whole, I should say that the restrictions of college life in England are far less dangerous than the absolute freedom of life in an American college. Under our system a few men profit greatly; they leave college experienced in the ways of the world and at the same time thoroughly masters of themselves. But it is a strong man — perhaps a blasphemous one — that would ask to be led into temptation. The best system of college residence, I take it, is that which develops thoroughly and spontaneously the normal social instincts, and at the same time leaves men free moral agents. In a rightly constituted fellow, in fact, the normal social life constitutes the only real freedom. Those frowning college walls, which we are disposed to regard as instruments of pedagogical tyranny, are the means of nourishing the normal social life, and are thus in effect the bulwarks of a freer system than is known to American universities.

VII

CLUB LIFE IN THE COLLEGE

AS a place for the general purposes of residence — eating and sleeping, work and play — the English college is clearly quite as well organized and equipped as any of the societies, clubs, or fraternities of an American university. And whereas these are in their very nature small and exclusive, the college is ample in size and is consciously and effectively inclusive; the very fact of living in it insures a well-ordered life and abundant opportunity for making friends. Yet within this democratic college one finds all sorts of clubs and societies, except those whose main purpose is residential, and these are obviously not necessary.

By far the larger proportion of the clubs are formed to promote the recognized undergraduate activities. No college is without athletic and debating clubs, and there are musical and literary clubs almost everywhere. Membership in all of them is little more than a formal expression of the fact that a man desires to row, play cricket or football, to debate, read Shakespeare, or play the fiddle. Yet they are all conducted with a degree of social amenity that to an American is as surprising as it is delightful.

The only distinctively social feature of the athletic clubs is the wine, which is given to celebrate the close of a successful season. A boating wine I remember was held in a severe and sombre old hall, built before Columbus sailed the ocean blue. It was presided over by a knot of the dons, ancient oarsmen, whose hearts were still in the sport. They sat on the dais, like the family of a baron of the Middle Ages, while the undergraduates sat about the tables like faithful retainers. All the sportsmen of the college were invited, and everybody made as much noise as he could, especially one of the boating men, who went to the piano and banged out a song of triumph he had written, while we all tumbled into the chorus. One of the fellows — I have always taken it as a compliment to my presence — improvised a cheer after the manner not unknown in America, which was given with much friendly laughter. " Quite jolly, is n't it! " he remarked, with the pride of authorship, " and almost as striking as your cry of ' Quack, quack, quack ! ' " He had heard the Yale men give their adaptation of the frog chorus at the athletic games between Oxford and Yale. About midnight the college butler passed a loving cup of mulled wine of a spicy smoothness to fill your veins with liquid joy. The recipe, I was told, had been handed down by the butlers of the college since the fourteenth century, being older than the hall in which we were drinking. I have no doubt it was the cordial Chaucer calls Ypocras, which seems to have brought joy to his warm old heart. After the loving cup had gone about, the fellows cleared away the tables and danced a stag. At this stage of the game the dons discreetly faded away, and the wine resolved itself into a good-natured rag in the quad that was ended only by daylight and the dean. I have seen many feasts to celebrate athletic victory and the breaking of training, but none as homelike and pleasant all through as the wine of an Oxford college.

The debating clubs have of necessity a distinct social element, for where there is much talk, food and drink will always be found; and with the social element there is apt to be some little exclusiveness. In Balliol there are three debating clubs, and they are of course in some sense rivals. Like the fraternities in an American college, they look over the freshmen each year pretty closely; and the freshmen in turn weigh the clubs. One freshman gave his verdict as follows: "The fellows in A are dull, and bathe; the fellows in B are clever, and sometimes bathe; the fellows in C are supposed to be clever." The saying is not altogether a pleasant one, but will serve to indicate the range of selection of members. In spite of social distinctions, few fellows need be excluded who care to debate or are clubable in spirit. As a system, the clubs are inclusive rather than exclusive.

Each club convenes at regular intervals, usually in the rooms of such members as volunteer to be hosts. The hour of meeting is directly after dinner, and while the men gather and settle down to the business of the evening, coffee, port, and tobacco are provided out of the club treasury. The debates are supposed to be carried on according to the strictest parliamentary law, and the man who transgresses is subject to a sharp rebuff. On one occasion, when the question of paying members of Parliament was up, one speaker gravely argued that the United States Senate was filled with politicians who were attracted by the salary. Though I had already spoken, I got up to protest. The chairman sat me down with the greatest severity — amid a broad and general smile. I had neglected, I suppose, the parliamentary remark that I arose to a point of fact. A member's redress in such instances is to rag the president at the time when, according to custom, interpellations are in order; and as a rule he avails himself of this opportunity without mercy. On one occasion, a fellow got up in the strictest parliamentary manner and asked the president — a famous shot on the moors — whether it was true, as reported, that on the occasion when he lately fell over a fence three wrens and a chipping sparrow fell out of his game-bag. Such ragging as the chair administers and receives may not aid greatly in rational debate, but it certainly has its value as a preparation for the shifts and formalities of parliamentary life. It is the first duty of a chairman, even the president of the Oxford Union, to meet his ragging with cheerfulness and a ready reply, and the first duty of all debaters is to be interesting as well as convincing. In American college debating there is little of such humor and none of such levity. The speakers are drafted to sustain or to oppose a position, often without much reference to their convictions, and are supposed to do so to the uttermost. The training is no doubt a good one, for life is largely partisan; but a man's success in the world depends almost as much on his tact and good sense as on his strenuosity.

The Englishman's advantage in address is sometimes offset by deficiencies of information. In a debate on Home Rule, one argument ran somewhat as follows: It is asserted that the Irish are irresponsible and lacking in the sense of administrative justice. To refute this statement, I have only to point to America, to the great metropolis of New York. There, as is well known, politics are exclusively in the hands of Irish citizens, who, denied the right of self-government — as the American colonies were denied similar freedom, I need scarcely point out with what disastrous results to the empire — the Irish immigrants in America, I say, are evincing their true genius for statesmanship in their splendid organization known as Tammany Hill.

In the better clubs, the debates are often well prepared and cogent. I remember with particular gratitude a discussion as to whether the English love of comfort was not an evidence of softening morals. The discussion was opened with a paper by a young Scotchman of family and fortune. More than any other man I met he had realized the sweetness and pleasantness of Oxford, and all the delights of the senses and of the mind that surround the fellows there; and the result of it was, as it has so often been with such men, a craving for the extreme opposite of all he had known, for moral earnestness and austerity. What right, he questioned, had one to buy a book which, with ever so little more effort, he might read in the Bodleian, while all the poor of England are uneducated? And was it manly or in any way proper to spend so much time and interest on things that are merely agreeable? The sense of the meeting seemed to be that comfort in daily life is an evil only when it becomes an end in itself, a self-indulgence; and that a certain amount of it is necessary to fortify one for the most strenuous and earnest work in the world. I think that debate made us realize, as we never could have realized without it, to what serious end England makes the ways of her young men so pleasant; yet the more deeply I lived into the life of the university, the more deeply I questioned, as the young Scotchman did, whether the line between the amenities and the austerities was not somewhat laxly drawn.

The only purely social club, and therefore the only really exclusive one, is the wine club. In Balliol there is a college rule against wine clubs, which seems to be due partly to a feeling against social exclusiveness, and partly perhaps to a distrust of purely convivial gatherings. The purpose of a wine club was served quite as well, however, by an organization that was ostensibly for debating. The notices of meetings were usually a parody of the notices of the meetings of genuine debating clubs, and the chief business of the secretary was to concoct them in pleasing variety. For instance, it would be *Resolved*, that this House looks with disfavor upon the gradual introduction of a continental sabbath into England; or *Resolved*, that this House looks with marked disfavor upon the assumption that total abstinence is a form of intemperance. On the evening when the House was defending total abstinence, our host's furniture and tea-things suffered some damage, and as I was in training, I found it advisable to leave early. As I slipped out, the president of the club, a young nobleman, who was himself at the time in training for the 'varsity trial eights, called me back and said with marked sobriety that he had just thought of something. "You are in for the mile run, are n't you? And in America you have always run the half. Well, then, if you find the distance too long for you, just don't mind at all about the first part of the race, but when you get to the last part, run as you run a half mile. Do it in two minutes, and you can't help beating 'em." He bade me good-night with a grave and authoritative shake of the hand. If he recalled his happy thought next morning, he was unable to avail himself of it, for I grieve to say that in the 'varsity trial race, which came only a few days later, he missed his blue by going badly to pieces on the finish.

The meeting at which this occurred was exceptional. For the most part the fellows were moderate enough, and at times I suspected the wine club of being dull. Certainly, we had no such fun as at the more general jubilations — a rag in the quad or a boating wine. I doubt if any one would have cared so very much to belong to the club if it had not afforded the only badge of social distinction in college, and if this had not happened to be an unusually pretty hatband. However successful a wine club may be, moreover, it is of far less consequence than similar clubs in America. In the first place, since there are one or more of them in each of the twenty colleges, the number of men who belong to them is far greater relatively, which of course means far less exclusion. In the second place, and this is more important, the fellows who do not belong are still able to enjoy the life which is common to all members of the college. In general, the social walls of Oxford are like the material ones. Far from being the means of undue exclusion and of the suppression of public feeling, they are the live tissues in which the vital functions of the place are performed.

Until well along in the nineteenth century, this

life in the college was about the only life; but of late years the university has begun to feel its unity more strongly, and in social and intellectual life, as in athletics, it has become for the first time since the Middle Ages an organic whole.

VIII

SOCIAL LIFE IN THE UNIVERSITY

THE first formal organization of the life of the university was, as its name records, the Oxford Union, an institution of peculiar interest to Americans because our universities, though starting from a point diametrically opposite, have arrived at a state of social disorganization no less pronounced than that which the Union was intended to remedy. Harvard, which has progressed farthest along the path of social expansion and disintegration, has already made a conscious effort to imitate the Union. The adamantine spirit of Yale is shaken by the problems of the Sophomore societies; and it will not be many decades before other universities will be in a similar predicament. It will not be amiss, therefore, to consider what the Oxford Union has been and is. If Americans have not clearly understood it even when attempting to imitate it, one should at least remember that it would not be easy for an Oxford man to explain it thoroughly.

The Union was founded in 1823, and was primarily for debating. In fact, it was the only university debating society. Its members were carefully selected for their ability in discoursing on the questions of the day. In its debates Gladstone, Lord Rosebery, the Marquis of Salisbury, and countless other English statesmen of recent times got their first parliamentary training. Its present fame in England is largely based upon this fact; but its character has been metamorphosed. Early in its history it developed social features; and though it was still exclusive in membership, little by little men of all kinds were taken in. At this stage of its development, the Union was not unlike those vast political clubs in London in which any and all principles are subordinated to the kitchen and the wine cellar. The debates, though still of first-rate quality, became more and more an incident; the club was chiefly remarkable as the epitome of all the best elements of Oxford life. The library was filled with men reading or working at special hobbies; the reading and smoking rooms were crowded; the lawn was daily thronged with undergraduates gossiping over a cup of tea; the telegram board, the shrine of embryo politicians watching for the results from a general election, was apt to be profaned by sporting men scanning it for the winners of the Derby or the Ascot. In a word, the Union held the elect of Oxford, intellectual, social, and sporting. This is the Union remembered by the older graduates, and except for a single feature, namely, that it was still exclusive, this is the Union that has inspired the projectors of the Harvard Union.

The Oxford man of the later day knows all too well that this Union is no more. Some years ago, responding to a democratic impulse that has been very strong of late at Oxford, the Union threw down all barriers; virtually any man nowadays may join it, and its members number well beyond a thousand. The result is not a social millennium. The very feature of inclusiveness that is to be most prominent in the Union at Harvard destroyed the character of the Oxford Union as a representative body. To the casual observer it still looks much as it did a dozen years ago; but its glory has departed. In any real sense of the word it is a Union no more. The men who used to give it character are to be found in smaller clubs, very much like the clubs of an American university.

The small university debating clubs are the Russell, the Palmerston, the Canning, and the Chatham, each of which stands for some special stripe of political thought, and each of which has a special color which — sure sign of the pride of exclusiveness — it wears in hatbands.   The clubs meet periodically — often weekly — in the rooms of members.   Sometimes a paper is read which is followed by an informal discussion ; but the usual exercise is a formal debate.   Time was when the best debates came off at the Union, and writers of leading articles in London papers even now look to it as a political weather-vane.   The debates there are still earnest and sometimes brilliant, and to have presided over them is a distinction of value in after life ; but as far as I could gather, their prestige is falling before the smaller debating clubs.   The main interest at the Union appeared to centre in the interpellation of the president, which is carried on much as in the House of Commons, though with this difference, that, following the immemorial custom, it is turned into ragging.   When this is over, the major part of the audience clears out to the smoking and reading rooms.   In the smaller clubs the exercises are not only serious, but — in spite of the preliminary ragging, which no function at Oxford may flourish without — they are taken seriously.   The clubs really include the best forensic ability of Oxford.   At the end of each year they give dinners, at which new and old members gather, while some prominent politician from Westminster holds forth on the question of the hour. In a word, these clubs, collectively, are what the Union once was — the training school of British statesmen.

The university social clubs are of a newness that shocks even an American; but it would not be quite just to account for the fact by regarding them as mere offshoots, like the debating clubs, of a parent Union. Until the nineteenth century, there really was no university at Oxford, at least in modern times. The colleges were quite independent of one another socially and in athletics, and each of them provided all the necessary instruction for its members. The social clubs which now admit members from the university at large began life as wine clubs of separate colleges, and even to-day the influence of the parent college is apt to predominate. The noteworthy fact is that in proportion as the social prestige of the Union has declined, these college wine clubs, like the small debating clubs, have gained character and prestige.

The oldest of these is the Bullingdon, which is not quite as old, I gathered, as the Institute of 1770 at Harvard, and, considered as a university organization, it is of course much younger. It was originally the Christ Church wine club, and to-day it is dominated by the sporting element of Christ

Church, which is the most aristocratic of Oxford colleges. In former years, it is said, the club had kennels at Bullingdon, and held periodic hunts there; and it is still largely composed of hunting men. To-day it justifies its name mainly by having an annual dinner beneath the heavy rafters of a mediæval barn at Bullingdon. On these, as on other state occasions, the members wear a distinctive costume — no doubt a tradition from the time when men generally wore colors — which consists of a blue evening coat with white facings and brass buttons, a canary waistcoat, and a blue tie. This uniform is no doubt found in more aristocratic wardrobes than any other Oxford trophy. The influence of the Bullingdon is indirectly to discourage athletics, which it regards as unaristocratic and incompatible with conviviality; so that Christ Church, though the largest of Oxford colleges and one of the wealthiest, is of secondary importance in sports. For this reason the Bullingdon has suffered a partial eclipse, for the middle-class spirit which is invading Oxford has given athletic sports the precedence over hunting, while expensive living and mere social exclusiveness are less the vogue. By a curious analogy, one of the oldest and most exclusive of the clubs at Harvard is similarly out of sympathy with the athletic spirit.

Another old and prominent college wine club that has come to elect members from without is the Phœnix of Brazenose, the uniform of which is perhaps more beautiful than the Bullingdon uniform, consisting of a peculiar dark wine-colored coat, brass buttons, and a light buff waistcoat. In general, the college wine clubs are more or less taking on a university character. The Annandale Club of Balliol, for instance, has frequent guests from outside, and often elects them to membership out of compliment. At the formal wines the members have the privilege of inviting outside guests.

The most popular and representative Oxford club is Vincent's, which owes its prominence to the fact that it expresses the enthusiasm of modern Oxford for athletics. It was founded only a third of a century ago, but it must be remembered that inter-varsity boat races did not become usual until 1839, nor a fixture until 1856; that the first inter-varsity athletic meeting came in 1864, and the first inter-varsity football game as late as 1873. Vincent's was originally composed largely of men from University College, which was at that time a leader in sports; but later it elected many men from Brazenose, then in the ascendant. When Brazenose became more prominent in athletics, it gained a controlling influence in Vincent's; and when it declined, as it lately did, the leadership passed on. The name Vincent's came from a printer's shop, above which the club had its rooms. Any second year man is eligible; in fact, until a few years ago, freshmen were often taken in. The limit of members is ninety, but as the club is always a dozen or so short of this, no good fellow is excluded for lack of a place. When a man is proposed, his name is written in a book, in which space is left for friends in the club to write their names in approval. After this, elections are in the hands of a committee. Like all Oxford clubs, Vincent's will always, I suppose, lean towards men of some special college or group of colleges; yet it is careful to elect all clubable blues, and, in point of fact, is representative of the university at large, as, for instance, the Hasty Pudding Club at Harvard, or the senior societies at Yale, to which, on the whole, it most nearly corresponds.

The most democratic, as well as one of the most recent of the more purely social clubs, is the Gridiron. It is a dining rather than a social club, and one may invite to his board as many guests who are not members as he chooses. Any good fellow is eligible, though here, again, a man in one of the less known colleges might fail to get in from lack of acquaintances on the election committee.

The Union has long lost prestige before this development of small exclusive clubs. Politically, socially, and even in that most essential department, the kitchen, it holds a second place. If you ask men of the kind that used to give it its character why they never go there, they will tell you, in the most considerate phrase, how the pressure of other undergraduate affairs is so great that they have not yet found time; and this is quite true. They may add that next year they intend to make the time, for they believe that one should know all kinds of men at Oxford; and they are quite sincere. But next year they are more preoccupied than ever. If Oxford is united socially, it is not because of the Oxford Union.

In addition to the clubs which are mainly social, there is the usual variety of special organizations. These, as a rule, are of recent growth. The Musical Union has frequent meetings for practice, and gives at least one concert a year. The Dramatic Society, the O. U. D. S., as it is popularly called, will be seen to be a very portentous organization. In America, college men give comic operas and burlesques, usually writing both the book and the music themselves; and when they do, there is apt to be a Donnybrook Fair for vulnerable heads in the faculty. So well is musical nonsense adapted to the calibre of the undergraduate mind that college plays sometimes find their way to the professional stage, and to no small general favor. At Oxford the Vice-Chancellor, who is a law to himself and to the university, has decreed that there shall be no fun and nonsense. If the absurdities of donnishness are all too fair a mark for the undergraduate wit, the Vice-Chancellor has found a very serviceable scapegoat. He permits the undergraduates to present the plays of Shakespeare. Surely Shakespeare can stand the racket. The aim of the O. U. D. S. seems to be to get as many blues as possible into the cast of a Shakespearean production, with the idea, perhaps, of giving Oxford its full money's worth. I remember well the sensation made by the most famous of all university athletes, — a " quadruple blue," who played on four university teams, was captain of three of them, and held one world's record. The play was " The Merchant of Venice," and the athlete in question was the swarthy Prince of Morocco. Upon opening the golden casket his powers of elocution rose to unexpected heights. Fellows went again and again to hear him cry, " O hell! what have we here?" In one way, however, the performances of the O. U. D. S. are really noteworthy. Not even the crudest acting can entirely disguise the influences of birth and environment; and few Shakespearean actors have as fine a natural carriage as those companies of trained athletes. For the first time, perhaps, on any stage, the ancient Roman honor more or less appeared in Antonio, and there were really two gentlemen in Verona. For this reason — or, what is more likely, merely because the plays are given by Oxford men — the leading dramatic critics of London run up every year for the O. U. D. S. performance, and talk learnedly about it in their dignified periodicals. Both the musical and the dramatic societies have an increasing social element, and the dramatic society has a house of its own.

Of at least one association I happened upon, I know of no American parallel. One Sunday afternoon, a lot of fellows who had been lunching each other in academic peace were routed from college by a Salvation Army gathering that was sending up the discordant notes of puritanical piety just outside the walls. In the street near by we came upon a quiet party of undergraduates in cap and gown. They were standing in a circle, at the foot of the Martyr's Memorial, and were alternately singing hymns and exhorting the townspeople who gathered about. Their faces were earnest and simple, their attitude erect. If they were conscious of doing an unusual thing, they did not show it. I don't remember that they moved any of us to repent the pleasantness of our ways, but I know that they filled the most careless of us with a very definite admiration. One of the fellows said that he thought them mighty plucky, and that they had the stuff at least out of which sportsmen are made. The phrase is peculiarly British, but in the undergraduate vernacular there is no higher epithet of praise. In America there are slumming societies and total abstinence leagues; but I never knew any body of men who had the courage to stand up in the highway and preach their gospel to passers-by.

IX

THE COLLEGE AND THE UNIVERSITY

THE distinctive feature of the social organization of Oxford life is said to be the colleges.
Fifty years ago the remark held good, but to-day
it requires an extension. The distinctive feature
is the duality of the social organization: a man
who enters fully into undergraduate affairs takes
part both in the life of the college and in the life
of the university. The life of the college, in so
far as it is wholesome, is open to all newcomers;
it is so organized as to exert powerfully upon
them the force of its best influences and traditions, and is thus in the highest degree inclusive.
The life of the university, in so far as it is vigorous, is in the main open only to those who bring
to it special gifts and abilities, and is therefore
necessarily exclusive. In college, one freely en-
joys all that is fundamental in the life of a young
man — a pleasant place to sleep in and to dine
in, pleasant fellows with whom to work and to
play. In the university, one finds scope for his
special capacities in conviviality or in things of

the mind. More than any other institution, the English university thus mirrors the conditions of social life in the world at large, in which one is primarily a member of his family, and takes part in the life of the outside community in proportion as his abilities lead him.

The happiest thing about all this is that it affords the freest possible interplay of social forces. As soon as a newcomer gains distinction, as he does at once if he has the capacity, he is noticed by the leading men of the college, and is thus in a way to be taken into the life of the university. From the college breakfast it is only a step to the Gridiron, from the college eight to Vincent's, and from the debating society to the Chatham or the Canning. These, like all undergraduate clubs, are in yearly need of new members, and the older men in college are only too glad to urge the just claims of the younger for good-fellowship sake, and for the general credit of their institution.

Even when a fellow has received all the university has to offer, he is still amenable to the duality of Oxford life. In American institutions, in proportion as a man is happily clubbed, he is by the very nature of the social organization withdrawn from his college mates; but at Oxford he still dines in Hall, holds forth at the college debating society, plays on the college teams, and, until his final year, he lives within the college walls. First, last, and always his general life is bound up with that of the college.

The prominent men thus become a medium by which every undergraduate is brought in touch with the life of the university. The news of the athletic world is reported at Vincent's over afternoon tea; and at dinner time the men who have discussed it there relate it to their mates in the halls of a dozen colleges. A celebrated debater brings the news of the Union or of the smaller clubs; and whatever a man's affiliations in the university, he can scarcely help bringing the report of them back with him. In an incredibly short time all undergraduate news, and the judgments upon it of those best qualified to judge, ramify the college; and men who seldom stir beyond its walls are brought closely in touch with the innermost spirit of the university life. Here, again, those forbidding walls make possible a freedom of social interplay which is unknown in America. The real union of Oxford, social, athletic, and intellectual, is quite apart from the so-called Oxford Union; it results from the nice adjustment between the general residential life of the colleges and the specialized activities of the university.

The immediate effect of this union is the humble one of making the present life of the undergraduate convenient and enjoyable; but its ultimate effect is a matter of no little importance. Every undergraduate, in proportion to his susceptibilities and capacities, comes under the influence of the social and intellectual traditions of Oxford, which are the traditions of centuries of the best English life. In Canada and Australia, South Africa and India, you will find the old Oxonian wearing the hatband, perhaps faded and weatherstained, that at Oxford denoted the thing he was most proud to stand for; and wherever you find him, you will find also the manners and standards of the university, which are quite as definite a part of him, though perhaps less conspicuous. Without a large body of men animated by such traditions, it is no exaggeration to say that it would not have been possible to build up the British empire. If the people of the United States are to bear creditably the responsibilities to civilization that have lately fallen to them, or have been assumed, there is urgent need for institutions that shall similarly impose upon our young men the best traditions and influences of American life.

II

OXFORD OUT OF DOORS

I

SLACKING ON THE ISIS AND THE CHERWELL

THE dual development of college and university, with all its organic coördinations, exists also in the sports of Oxford. The root and trunk of the athletic spirit lies in the colleges, though its highest development is found in university teams. To an American, this athletic life of the college will be found of especial interest, for it is the basis of the peculiar wholesomeness and moderation of Oxford sports. If the English take their pleasures sadly, as they have been charged with doing ever since Froissart hit upon the happy phrase, they are not so black a pot but that they are able to call us blacker; in the light of international contests, they have marveled at the intensity with which our sportsmen pursue the main chance. The difference here has a far deeper interest than the critic of boating or track athletics often realizes. Like the songs of a nation, its sports have a definite relation to its welfare: one is tempted to say, Let me rule the games of my countrymen and who will may frame their laws. At least, I hope to

be pardoned if I speak with some particularity of
the out-of-door life, and neglect the lofty theme
of inter-varsity contests for the humbler pursuits
of the common or garden undergraduate.

The origin of the boating spirit is no doubt
what the Oxonian calls slacking, for one has to
learn to paddle in a boat before he can row to
advantage ; and in point of fact the bumping races
are supposed to have originated among parties of
slackers returning at evening from up the river.
If I were to try to define what a slacker is, I suppose you could answer that all Oxford men are
slackers; but there are depths beneath depths of
far niente. The true slacker avoids the worry and
excitement of breakfast parties and three-day
cricket matches, and conserves his energies by
floating and smoking for hours at a time in his
favorite craft on the Isis and the Cherwell — or
"Char," as the university insists on calling it. He
is a day-dreamer of day-dreamers ; and despised as
he is by the more strenuous Oxford men, who yet
stand in fear of the fascination of his vices, he is
as restful a figure to an American as a negro bask-
ing on a cotton-wharf, and as appealing as a beggar steeped in Italian sunlight. Merely to think
of his uninterrupted calm and his insatiable appe-
tite for doing nothing is a rest to occidental

nerves; and though one may never be a roustabout and loaf on a cotton-wharf, one may at any time go to Oxford and play through a summer's day at slacking.

Before you come out, you must make the acquaintance of the O. U. H. S. — that is, the University Humane Society. In the winter, when there is skating, the Humane Society man stands by the danger spot with a life-buoy and a rope; and in the summer, when the streams swarm with pleasure-craft, he wanders everywhere, pulling slackers out of the Isis and the Char. In view of the fact that, metaphorically speaking at least, you can shake hands with your neighbors across either of these streams, the Humane Society man is not without his humors.

You may get yourself a tub or a working-boat or a wherry, a rob-roy or a dinghy, for every craft that floats is known on the Thames; but the favorite craft are the Canadian canoe and the punt. The canoe you will be familiar with, but your ideas of a punt are probably derived from a farm-built craft you have poled about American duck-marshes — which bears about the same relationship to this slender, half-decked cedar beauty that a canal-boat bears to a racing-shell.

During your first perilous lessons in punting,

you will probably be in apprehension of ducking your mentor, who is lounging among the cushions in the bow. But you cannot upset the punt any more than you can discompose the Englishman; the punt simply upsets you without seeming to be aware of it. And when you crawl dripping up the bank, consoled only by the fact that the Humane Society man was not at hand with his boat-hook to pull you out by the seat of the trousers, your mentor will gravely explain how you made your mistake. Instead of bracing your feet firmly on the bottom and pushing with the pole, you were leaning on the pole and pushing with your feet. When the pole stuck in the clay bottom, of course it pulled you out of the boat.

Steering is a matter of long practice. When you want to throw the bow to the left, you have only to pry the stern over to the right as you are pulling the pole out of the water. To throw the bow to the right, ground the pole a foot or so wide of the boat, and then lean over and pull the boat up to it. That is not so easy, but you will learn the wrist motion in time. When all this comes like second nature, you will feel that you have become a part of the punt, or rather that the punt has taken life and become a part of you.

A particular beauty of punting is that, more

A RACING PUNT AND PUNTER

than any other sport, it brings you into personal contact, so to speak, with the landscape. In a few days you will know every inch of the bottom of the Char, some of it perhaps by more intimate experience than you desire. Over there, on the outer curve of the bend, the longest pole will not touch bottom. Fight shy of that place. Just beyond here, in the narrows, the water is so shallow that you can get the whole length of your body into every sweep. As for the shrubbery on the bank, you will soon learn these hawthorns, if only to avoid barging into them. And the Magdalen chestnut, which spreads its shade so beautifully above the water just beyond, becomes quite familiar when its low-reaching branches have once caught the top of your pole and torn it from your hands.

The slackers you see tied up to the bank on both sides of the Char are always here after luncheon. An hour later their craft will be as thick as money-bugs on the water, and the joys of the slackers will be at height. You won't, as a rule, detect happiness in their faces, but it is always obvious in the name of the craft. One man calls his canoe "Vix Satis," which is the mark the university examining board uses to signify that a man's examination paper is a failure. Another has

"P. T. O." on his bows — the "Please Turn Over" which an Englishman places at the bottom of a card where we say "Over." Still another calls his canoe the "Non-conformist Conscience" — which, as you are expected to remark, is very easily upset. All this makes the slacker even happier than if he were so un-English as to smile his pleasure, for he has a joke ready-made on his bow, where there is no risk of any one's not seeing it.

These pollard willows that line the bank are not expected to delight your eye at first sight, but as you see them day after day, they grow on you like the beauty of the bull-terrier pup that looks at you over the gunwale of the boat tied beneath them. They have been topped to make their roots strike deeper and wider into the soil, so that when the freshets come in the spring the banks will stand firm. The idea came some centuries ago from Holland, but has been so thoroughly Englished that the university, and, indeed, all England, would scarcely be itself without its pollard willows. And though the trees are not in themselves graceful, they make a large part of the beauty of the river scenery. The sun is never so golden as up there among their quivering leaves, and no shadow is so deep as that in the water at their feet.

The bar of foam ahead of us is the overflow

from the lasher — that is to say, from the still
water above the weir. The word " lasher " is obsolete almost everywhere else in England, and even
to the Oxford mind it describes the lashing overflow rather than the *lache* or *slack* water above.
When we " shoot the lasher," as the phrase goes,
you will get a hint as to why the obsolete term
still clings to this weir. Those fellows beyond
who have tied up three deep to the bank are
waiting to see us get ducked; but it is just as
easy to shoot the lasher as to upset in it; and
with that swarm of slackers watching, it makes a
difference which you do. We have only to get up
a fair pace and run into it on a diagonal. The
lashing torrent will catch our bows, but we shall
be half over before it sweeps them quite around;
and then it will catch the stern in turn, and whirl
the bow back into the proper direction. A sudden lurching of the bow, the roaring of a torrent
beneath, a dash of spray — and we are in still
water again.

In order to reach the inn at Marston by four we
must pole on. If we were true slackers, to be sure,
we should have brought a spirit lamp and a basket
of tea, and tied up in the first convenient nook on
the bank; but these are heights of slacking to
which the novice cannot aspire. Just beyond here

we shall have to give the Thames Conservancy man threepence to roll the punt around a weir. If there were ladies with us, we should have to let them walk a quarter of a mile on shore, for just above is Parson's Pleasure, the university bathing-hole; and these men, who would not let the Yale and the Cornell athletes appear in sleeveless "zephyrs," plunge into a frequented waterway without any zephyrs at all.

Above Parson's Pleasure we emerge from Mesopotamia — as the pretty river bottom is called in which the Char divides into several channels — and come in sight of the 'varsity cricket-ground. There is a game on against a picked eleven from the Marylebone Club; and every few minutes, if we waited, we might see the statuesque figures in white flannel suddenly dash after a ball or trot back and forth between the wickets. Few slackers have had energy to get beyond this point; and as we pole among the meadows, the cuckoo's homely voice emphasizes the solitude, singing the same two notes it sang to Shakespeare — and to Chaucer before him, for the matter of that.

At Marston, having ordered tea of the red-cheeked housewife, it is well to ask the innkeeper for credit. He is a Parisian, whose sociological principles, it is said, were the cause of his venturing across the Channel — in Paris, a man will even go as far as that for his opinions; and while his cheery English spouse, attended by troops of his red-cheeked boys, brings out the thin buttered bread, he will revile you. What business have you to ask an honest yeoman to lend you money? If he were to go down to Oxford and ask the first gentleman he met to lend him half a crown to feed his starving family, should he get it? Should he? And what right have you to come to his house — his *home!* — and demand food at his board? You are a gentleman; but what is a gentleman? A gentleman is the dregs of the idleness of centuries! Then he will declaim about his plans for the renovation of the world. All this time his well-fed wife has been pouring out the tea and slicing the Genoa cake; and now, with a smile of reassurance, she takes our names and college. But the innkeeper's eloquence does not flag, and it will not until you tell him with decision that you have had enough. This you are loath to do, for he has furnished you with a new ideal of happiness. The cotton-wharf negro sometimes wants leisure, the repose of the cricketer is at times rudely broken in upon, and even the slacker is liable to his ducking; but to stand up boldly against the evils of the world and to picture the new Utopia while your wife averts all practical consequences, this is *otium cum dignitate.*

This journey up the Char, though all-popular with the undergraduate, is not the only one worth taking. We might have gone down the Isis to the Iffley Mill and the sleepy little Norman church near by. This would have taken us through the thick of the college crews training for the summer eights. But the rules of the river are so complicated that no man on earth who has not given them long hours of study can understand them; and if an eight ran into us, we should be fined a quid or two — one quid for a college eight, and two for the 'varsity. Below Iffley, indeed, there is as much clear punting as you could desire, and here you are in the full current of Thames pleasure-boats. The towing-path skirts the water, so that when you are tired of punting you can get out and tow your craft. The stretch of river here I hold memorable as the scene of the only bit of dalliance I ever witnessed in this most sentimental of environments. A young man and a young woman had tied the painter of their punt to the middle of a paddle, and shoulder by shoulder were loitering along the river-side. Twenty yards behind, three other men and a baffled chaperon were steering the punt clear of the bank, and boring one another.

IFFLEY LOCK AND MILL

SLACKING

The best trip on the Isis is into the backwaters. These are a mesh of tiny streams that break free from the main current above Oxford and lose themselves in the broad bottom-lands. The islands they form were chosen in the Dark Ages as the sites of religious houses; for not only was the land fertile, but the network of deep, if tiny, streams afforded defense from the heathen, while the main channel of the Thames afforded communication with the Christian world. The ruins of these, or of subsequent monasteries, remain to-day brooding over a few Tudor cottages and hamlets, with a mill and a bakery and an inn or two to sustain life in the occasional undergraduate who lazes by in his canoe.

The most interesting of these ruins is Wytham. The phrase is exact, for the entire hamlet was built from a venerable religious house shortly after the dissolution of the monasteries. You can imagine the size of Wytham. If you don't watch very closely as you paddle up the sedgy backwater, you will miss it entirely, and that would be a pity, for its rude masonry, thatched roofs, and rustic garden fronts seem instinct with the atmosphere of Tudor England. The very tea roses, nodding languidly over the garden wall, smell, or seem to smell, as subtly sweet as if they had been pressed for ages between the leaves of a mediæval romance.

I am not quite sure that they do, though, for these ancient hamlets have strange ways of pulling the wool — a true golden fleece, to be sure — over American eyes. Once at twilight I heard a knot of strolling country men and women crooning a tune which was so strangely familiar that I immediately set it down as a village version of one of the noble melodies of that golden age when English feeling found its natural vent in song. As it drew nearer, I suddenly recognized it. It was a far-away version of " Mammy's Little Alabama Coon."

I have still faith, though, in a certain mediæval barmaid I chanced upon in the backwaters. The circumstances of our meeting were peculiar. As I drifted along one Sunday, perched on an after-thwart of the canoe, the current swept me toward a willow that leaned over the water, and I put up my hand to fend off. I chanced to be laughing to myself at the time at the thought of a fellow who, only the day before at the lasher, had tried to do the same thing. The lasher was forcing his punt against the willow on the opposite bank, where-upon, to my heart's delight, he lazily tried to fend it off with his arms. The punt refused to be fended off, and he stooped with an amusing effect of deliberation plump into the water. He was hauled out by the O. U. H. S. man hard by.

I was interrupted in these pleasant reminiscences by the roaring of waters about my ears, mingled with a boorish guffaw from one of the fellows behind me. . . . But I started to tell about the mediæval barmaid. Making my way to a bakehouse up the stream, I hung my coat and trousers before the fire on a long baker's pole, and put my shoes inside the oven on a dough tray. My companion of the horse-laugh hung my shirt on a blossoming almond-tree, and then left for the lunch hamper. He had scarcely gone when I heard the rustle of skirts at the door. " What do you want? " I cried. " I want my dinner," was the friendly reply. It was the barmaid of a neighboring public house, in her Sunday frock.

When she saw me she smiled, but maintained a dignity of port that — I insist upon it — was instinct with the simple and primitive modesty of the Middle Ages. It was the modesty of the people before whom Adam in the Chester mystery play was required by the stage directions to " stand nakyd and not be ashamyd." My barmaid advised me to take off my stockings and hang them up before the fire. The advice I admit came as a shock, but on reflection I saw that it was capital. For one happy moment I lived in the broad, wholesome atmosphere of the Middle Ages. It was like a breath from Chaucer's England.

Then the baker rushed into the room, in a cut-away Sunday coat of the latest style. He had baked for an Oxford college so long that he had become infected with the squeamish leaven of the nineteenth century. He called the girl a huzzy, and, taking her by the shoulder, hustled her into the garden, and then passed her plum pudding out to her gingerly through a crack in the door. He covered me with apologies and a bath-robe; but I did not mind either, for as the barmaid ran back to the inn she was laughing what I still insist upon believing to have been the simple joyous laughter of the Middle Ages.

But we must hurry to get back to college in time for dinner. And even at that we shall have to stop here at Magdalen bridge and give a street boy sixpence to take the punt the rest of the way. We land at the foot of the tower just as the late afternoon sun is gilding its exquisite pinnacles, and the chimes in its belfry are playing the prelude to the hour of seven. It is a melody worth all the Char and the Isis, with all their weirs and their willows. Other mediæval chimes fill you with a delicious sorrow for the past; but when they cease, and the great bell tolls out the hour, you think only of the death of time. It leaves you sadly beneath the tower, in the musty cellarage. But the melody that the Magdalen chimes utter is full of the fervid faith, the aspirations, of our fathers. It lifts you among the gilded pinnacles, or perhaps ever so little above them.

II

AS SEEN FROM AN OXFORD TUB

TO the true slacker, the college barges that
line the Isis are an object of aversion, for
into them sooner or later every fellow who loves
the water finds his way, and then there is an end
of slacking. Each of the barges is a grammar
school of oarsmanship, where all available men are
taught everything, from what thickness of leather
to wear on the heels of their boating-shoes to the
rhythm in rowing by which alone an eight can
realize its full speed; and from the barges issues
a navy of boats and boating-men more than ten
times as large as that of an American university.
When Mr. R. C. Lehmann arrived at Cambridge
to coach the Harvard crew, he was lost in admiration of the Charles River and the Back Bay, and
in amazement at the absence of boats on them. At
either Yale or Harvard it would be easy to give
space to both of the fleets that now swarm on the
slender Isis and threadlike Cam. We have water
enough — as a Congressman once remarked of our
fighting navy — it is only the boats that are lack-

ing. The lesson we have to learn of our English cousins is not so much a matter of reach and swing, outrigger and blades, as a generous and wholesome interest in boating for the sake of the boat and of the water; and it is less apparent in an Oxford 'varsity eight than in the humblest tub of the humblest college.

The first suggestion that I should go out to be tubbed came from the gray-bearded dean of the college, who happened at the time to be taking me to the master for formal presentation. I told him that I had tried for my class crew, and that three days on the water had convinced the coach that I was useless. He fell a pace behind, looked me over, and said that I might at least try. As this was his only advice, I did not forget it; and when my tutor, before advising me as to my studies, also urged me to row, I gave the matter some serious thought.

I found subsequently that every afternoon, between luncheon and tea, the college was virtually deserted for field, track, and river; and it dawned upon me that unless I joined the general exodus I should temporarily become a hermit. Still, my earlier unhappy experience in rowing was full in mind, and I set out for the barge humble in spirit, and prepared to be cursed roundly for three days, and "kicked out," or, as they say in Oxford, "given the hoof," on the fourth.

Few memories could be so unhappy, however, as to resist the beauty of the banks of the Isis. At New Haven, the first impression an oarsman gets is said to be an odor so unwelcome that it is not to be endeared even by four years of the good-fellowship and companionship of a Yale crew. At Harvard, the Charles — "Our Charles," as Longfellow spoke of it in a poem to Lowell — too often presents aspects which it would be sacrilege to dwell on. What the "royal-towered Thame" and "Camus, reverend sire," may have been in the classic days of English poetry it is perhaps safest not to inquire; suffice it that to-day they are — and especially the Thames — all that the uninitiated imagine "our Charles." Nowhere does the sun stream more cheerfully through the moist gray English clouds; nowhere is the grass more green, the ivy more luxuriant, and the pollard willows and slender elms and poplars more dense in foliage. And every building, from the thatched farm-cottage in Christ Church meadow to the Norman church at Iffley, is, as it were, more native and more a part of creation than the grass and trees. The English oarsman, it is true, cannot be as conscious of all this as an American visitor. Yet the love of outdoors, which has been at work for centuries in beautifying the English landscape, is not the least part of the British sporting instinct. Where an American might loiter in contemplation of these woods, fields, and streams, an Englishman shoots, hunts, crickets, and rows in them.

When you enter the barge on the river, you feel keenly the contrast with the bare, chill boat-houses of the American universities. On the centre tables are volumes of photographs of the crews and races of former years; the latest sporting papers are scattered on chairs and seats; and in one corner is a writing-table, with note-paper stamped " Balliol Barge, Oxford." There is a shelf or two of bound " Punches," and several shelves of books — " Innocents Abroad " and " Indian Summer," beside " Three Men in a Boat " and " The Dolly Dialogues." On the walls are strange and occult charts of the bumping races from the year one — which, if I remember rightly, is 1837. At the far end of the room is a sea-coal fire, above which shines the prow of a shell in which the college twice won the Ladies' Plate at Henley.

The dressing-room of the barge is sacred to the members of the eight, who at the present season are engaged in tubbing the freshmen in the hope of finding a new oar or two. At the appointed hour they appear, in eightsman blazers if it is fair, or in sou'westers if it is not — sad to relate, it usually is not — and each chooses a couple of men and leads them out to the float. Meanwhile, with the rest of the candidates — freshmen, and others who in past years have failed of a place in the torpids — you lounge on easy-chairs and seats, reading or chatting, until your own turn comes to be tubbed. It is all quiet like a club, except that the men are in full athletic dress.

The athletic costume is elaborate, and has been worn for a generation — since top-hats and trousers were abandoned, in fact — in more or less its present form. It consists of a cotton zephyr, flannel shorts flapping about the knees, and socks, or in winter Scotch hose gartered above the calves. The sweater, which, in cold weather, is worn on the river, has a deep V neck, supplemented when the oarsman is not in action by a soft woolen scarf or cloud. Over all are worn a flannel blazer and cap embroidered with the arms of the college. This uniform, with trifling variations, is used in all sports on field and river, and it is infinitely more necessary, in undergraduate opinion, than the academic cap and gown which the rules of the university require to be worn after dark. This seemingly elaborate dress is in effect the most

THE FULL COSTUME OF AN EIGHTSMAN

sensible in the world, and is the best expression I know of the cheerful and familiar way in which an Englishman goes about his sports. Reduced to its lowest terms. it is no more than is required by comfort and decency. With the addition of sweater, scarf, blazer, and cap, it is presentable in social conversation — indeed, in the streets of the city. It is in consequence of this that an afternoon in the barge is — except for the two tubbings on the river — so much like one spent in a club.

In America an oarsman wears socks and trunks which are apt to be the briefest possible. If he wears a shirt at all, it is often a mere ribbon bounding the three enormous apertures through which he thrusts his neck and shoulders. Before going on the river he is likely to shiver, in spite of the collar of his sweater; and after he comes in, his first thought is necessarily of donning street clothes. There is, in consequence, practically no sociability in rowing until the crews are selected and sent to the training-table. A disciple of Sartor Resartus would be very likely to conclude that, until American rowing adapts itself to the English costume, it must continue to be — except for the fortunate few — the bare, unkindly sport it has always been.

All this time I have had you seated in an armchair beside the sea-coal fire. Now an eightsman comes into the barge with two deep-breathing freshmen, and nods us to follow him to the boat the three have just quitted. On a chair by the door as we go out are several pads, consisting of a rubber cloth faced with wool. These are *spongeo pilenes*, or so I was told, which in English are known as Pontius Pilates — or Pontiuses for short. The eightsman will advise you to take a Pontius to protect your white flannel shorts from the water on the seat; for there is always a shower threatening, unless indeed it is raining. Every one knows, however, including the eightsman, that the wool is a no less important part of the Pontius than the rubber: it will save you many painful impressions of the dinner form in hall.

We are already on the river, and pair-oars, fours, and eights are swarming about us. "Come forward," cries our coach, "ready — paddle!" and we take our place in the procession of craft that move in one another's wake down the narrow river. The coach talks pleasantly to us from time to time, and in the course of an afternoon we get a pretty good idea of what the English stroke consists in.

The sun bursts through the pearl-gray clouds, and glows in golden ponds on the dense verdure of grass and trees. "Eyes in the boat," shouts the stern voice of conscience; but the coach says, "See, fellows. Here's a 'varsity trial eight. Watch them row, and you will see what the stroke looks like. Those fellows in red caps belong to the Leander."

Their backs are certainly not all flat, and to an American eye the crew presents a ragged appearance as a whole; but a second glance shows that every back swings in one piece from the hips, and that the apparent raggedness is due to the fact that the men on the bow side swing in one line, while those on the stroke side swing in another parallel line. They sway together with absolute rhythm and ease, and the boat is set on a rigidly even keel. Our coach looks them over critically, especially his three college-mates, one of whom at least he hopes will be chosen for the 'varsity eight. No doubt he aimed at a blue himself two years ago, when he came up; but blues are not for every man, even of those who row well and strongly. He watches them until they are indistinguishable amid the myriad craft in the distance. "It's jolly fine weather," he concludes pleasantly, with a familiar glance at the sky, which you are at liberty to follow. "Come forward. Ready — paddle!" We are presently in the barge again with the other fellows. A repetition of this experience after half an hour ends the day's work.

When I tried for the freshman crew in America, I was put with seven other unfortunates into a huge clinker barge, in charge of the sophomore coxswain. On the first day I was told to mind the angle on my oar. On the second day I was told to keep my eyes in the boat, damn me! On the third day, the sophomore coxswain wrought himself into a fury, and swore at me for not keeping the proper angle. When I glanced out at my blade he yelled, "Damn you, eyes in the boat!" This upset me so that I forgot thereafter to keep a flat back at the finish of the stroke. When we touched the float he jumped out, looked at my back, brought his boot against it sharply, and told me that there was no use in trying to row unless I could hold a flat back and swing my body between my knees. That night I sat on a dictionary with my feet against the footboard and tried to follow these injunctions, until my back seemed torn into fillets, but it would not come flat. I never went down to the river again, and it was two years before I summoned courage to try another sport. The bullyragging sophomore coxswain I came to know very well in later years, and found him as courteous and good-hearted as any man. To this day, if I mention our first meeting, he looks shy, and says he does n't remember it. He says that the flat back is a discarded fetish in Harvard boating circles, that even before the advent of Mr. Lehmann cursing and kicking were largely abandoned; and moreover (*fortissimo*) that the freshman crew he helped to curse and kick into shape was the only one in ten years that won.

After a fortnight's tubbing in pair-oars, the better candidates are tubbed daily in fours, and the autumn races are on the horizon. At the end of another week the boats are finally made up, and the crews settle down to the task of " getting together." Each of the fours has at least one seasoned oarsman to steady it, and is coached from the coxswain's seat by a member of the college eight. Sometimes, if the November floods are not too high, the coach runs or bicycles along the towing-path, where he can see the stroke in profile. If a coach swears at his men, there is sure to have been provocation. His favorite figure of speech is sarcasm. At the end of a heart-breaking burst he will say, " Now, men, get ready to *row*," or, " I say, fellows, wake up; *can't you make a difference?*" The remark of one coach is now a tradition — " All but four of you men are rowing badly, and they 're rowing damned badly ! " This convention of sarcasm is by no means old. One of the notable personages in Eights' Week is a little man who is pointed out to you as the Last of the Swearing Coaches. *Tempora mutantur.* Perhaps my friend the ex-coxswain is in line for a similar distinction.

When the fours are once settled in their tubs, the stroke begins to go much better, and the daily paddle is extended so as to be a real test of strength and endurance for the new men, and for the man from the torpid a brisk practice spin. Even at this stage very few of the new men are " given the hoof ; " the patience of the coachers is monumental.

The tubbing season is brought to an end with a race between the fours. Where there are half a dozen fours in training, two heats of three boats each are rowed the first day, and the finals between the best two crews on the following day. The method of conducting these races is characteristic of boating on the Isis and the Cam. As the river is too narrow to row abreast, the crews start a definite distance apart, and row to three flags a mile or so up the river, which are exactly as far apart as the boats were at starting. At each of these flags an eightsman is stationed. In

THE COLLEGE BARGES : TUBBING IN NOVEMBER FLOODS

the races I saw they flourished huge dueling pistols, and when the appropriate crew passed the flag, the appropriate man let off his pistol. The crew that is first welcomed with a pistol-shot wins. These races are less exciting than the bumping races; yet they have a picturesque quality of their own, and they settle the question of superiority with much less rowing. The members of the winning four get each a pretty enough prize to remember the race by, and the torpidsman at stroke holds the "Junior fours cup" for the year.

The crowning event of the season of tubbing is a wine, to which are invited all boating-men in college, and the representative athletes in other sports. In Balliol it is called the "Morrison wine," as the races are called "Morrison fours," in honor of an old Balliol man, a 'varsity oar and coach, who established the fund for the prizes. The most curious thing about this affair is that it is not given, as it would be in America, at the expense of the college, or even of the men who have been tubbed, but at the expense of those who are finally chosen to row in the races.

To my untutored mind the hospitality of English boating seemed a pure generosity. It made me uncomfortable at first, with the sense that I could never repay it; but I soon got over this, and basked in it as in the sun. The eightsmen devote their afternoons to coaching you because there are seats to be filled in the torpid and in the eight; they speak decently because they find that in the long run decency is more effective; and they hold the wine because they wish to honor the sport in which they have chosen to stake their reputations as athletes. In a word, where in America we row by all that is self-sacrificing and loyal, in England the welfare of boating is made to depend upon its attractiveness as a recreation and a sport; if it were not enjoyable to the normal man, nothing could force fellows into it.

The relationship of the autumn tubbing and its incidental sociability to the welfare of the sport in the college and in the university seems remote enough to the American mind, for out of the score of fellows who are tubbed only three or four, on an average, go farther in the sport. Yet it is typical of the whole; and it will help us in following the English boating season. Throughout the year there are two converging currents of activity in boating. On the one hand, the tubs in the autumu term develop men for the torpids, which come on during the winter term; and the torpids develop men for the summer eights. On the other hand, the 'varsity trials in the autumn term develop men for the 'varsity eight, which trains and races in the winter term ; and the 'varsity oarsmen, like the men who have prospered in tubs and torpids, end the season in the eights of their respective colleges. The goal of both the novice and the veteran is thus the college eight.

The torpid is, so to speak, the understudy to the college eight. In order to give full swing to the new men, no member of the eight of the year before is allowed to row in it ; and the leading colleges man two torpids — sometimes even three. The training here is much more serious than in the tubs ; wine, spirits, and tobacco are out of order. The races, which are conducted like the celebrated May Eights, are rowed in midwinter — in the second of the three Oxford terms — under leaden skies, and sometimes with snow piled up along the towing-path. On the barges, instead of the crowds of ladies, gayly dressed and bent on a week of social enjoyment, one finds knots of loyal partisans who are keen on the afternoon's sport. The towing-path, too, is not so crowded as in May Week ; but nothing could surpass the din of pistols and rattles and shouting that accompanies the races. If the men in the torpid do not learn how to row the stroke to the finish under the excitement of a race, it is not for the lack of coaching and experience. When the torpids break training, there are many ceremonies to signalize the return to the flesh-pots: one hardly realizes that the weeks of sport and comradeship have all gone to the filling of a place or two in the college eight.

All this time, while the tubs and torpids have been training up new men, the 'Varsity Boat Club, whose home is on the shore of the Isis opposite the row of college barges, has also, so to speak, been doing its tubbing. The new men for the 'varsity are chiefly those who have come to the front in the May Eights of the previous year — oars of two or three seasons' standing; though occasionally men are taken directly from the Eton eight, which enters yearly for the Ladies' Plate at Henley. The new men will number ten or a dozen; and early in the autumn they are taken out in tubs. They are soon joined by as many of last year's blues as are left in Oxford. The lot is divided into two eights, as evenly matched as possible, which are coached separately. These are called the Trial Eights, or 'Varsity Trials. To "get one's trials" is no mean honor. It is the *sine qua non* of membership to the Leander — admittedly the foremost boating club of the world. Toward the end of the first term there is a race of two and a half miles between the two trial eights at Moulsford, where the Thames is wide enough to permit the two boats to race abreast. Of the men who row in the trials the best ten or a dozen are selected to train for the 'varsity during the winter term.

Of the training of the 'varsity eight it is not necessary to speak here at length. The signal fact is that the men are so well schooled in the stroke, and so accustomed to racing, that a season of eight weeks at Oxford and at Putney is enough to fit them to go over the four miles and a quarter between Putney and Mortlake with the best possible results. The race takes place in March, just after the close of the winter term.

The series of races I have mentioned gives some idea of the scheme and scope of English boating, but it is by no means exhaustive. The strength of the boating spirit gives rise to no end of casual and incidental races. Chief among these are the coxswainless fours, which take place about the middle of the autumn term, while the trials are on the river. The crews are from the four or five chief boating colleges, and are made up largely from the men in the 'varsity trials. The races have no relation that I could discover to the 'varsity race ; the only point is to find which college has the best four, and it is characteristic that merely for the sport of it the training of the 'varsity trials is interrupted.

After the 'varsity race the members of the crew rest during what remains of the Easter vacation, and then take their places in the boats of their respective colleges. Here they are joined by the other trials men, the remaining members of last year's college eight, and the two or three men who have come up from the torpids. Now begins the liveliest season in boating. Every afternoon the river is clogged with eights rowing to Iffley or to Sandford, and the towing-path swarms with enthusiasts. The course in the May bumping races is a mile and a quarter long — the same as the course of the torpids — and the crews race over it every day for a week, with the exception of an intervening Sunday, each going up a place or down a place in the procession daily according as it bumps or is bumped. These races, from the point of view of the expert oarsman, are far less important than the 'varsity race; yet socially they are far more prominent, and the enthusiasm they arouse among the undergraduates is incomparable. The vitality of Oxford is in the colleges: the university organizations are the flowers of a very sturdy root and branch.

THE LAST DAY OF THE BUMPING RACES OF THE SUMMER EIGHTS (1895)

The difference between American and English boating is that we lack the root and branches of the college system. In a university of from three to four thousand men there are, in addition to the 'varsity crew, four class crews and perhaps a few scratch crews. In England, each of the score of colleges, numbering on an average something like one hundred and fifty men apiece, mans innumerable fours, one or more eight-oared torpids, and the college eight. A simple calculation will show that with us one man in fifty to seventy goes in for the sport, while in England the proportion is one man in five to seven.

The difference in spirit is as great as the difference in numbers. In America, the sole idea in athletics, as is proclaimed again and again, is to beat the rival team. No concession is made to the comfort or wholesomeness of the sport; men are induced to train by the excellent if somewhat grandiose sentiment that they owe it to the university to make every possible sacrifice of personal pleasure. Our class crews, which have long ceased to represent any real class rivalry, are maintained mainly in the hope of producing 'varsity material. The result of these two systems is curiously at variance with the intention. At Oxford, where rowing is very pleasant indeed, and where for the greater part of the year the main interest centres in college crews, the 'varsity reaches a high degree of perfection, and the oarsmen, without quite being aware of the fact, represent their university very creditably; while at Yale, and until recently at·Harvard, the subsidiary crews have been comparative failures in producing material, and the 'varsity is in consequence somewhat in the position of an exotic, being kept alive merely by the stimulus of inter-varsity rivalry.

The recent improvement at Harvard is due to Mr. Rudolph C. Lehmann, the celebrated Cambridge and Leander oar who coached the Harvard crews of 1897 and 1898, in the sportsmanlike endeavor to stimulate a broader and more expert interest in boating. His failure to bring either of the crews to victory, which to so many of us signified the utter failure of his mission, has had more than a sufficient compensation in the fact that he established at Harvard something like the English boating system. Anything strictly similar to the torpids and eights is of course out of the question, because we have no social basis such as the colleges afford for rivalry in boating; but the lack of colleges has in a measure been remedied by creating a factitious rivalry between improvised boating clubs, and the system of torpids and eights has been crudely imitated in the so-called graded crews. A season of preliminary racing has thus been established, on the basis of which the candidates for the 'varsity crew are now selected, so that instead of the nine months of slogging in the tank and on the river, in which the more nervous and highly organized candidates were likely to succumb and the stolid men to find a place in the boat, the eight is made up as at Oxford of those who have shown to best advantage in a series of spirited races. Crude as the new Harvard system is as compared with the English system, it has already created a true boating spirit, and has trained a large body of men in the established stroke, placing the sport at Harvard on a sounder basis than at any other American university. It has thus been of infinitely more advantage, by the potentiality of an example, than any number of victories at New London. To realize the full benefit of the system of graded crews and preliminary races, it is only necessary to supersede the arbitrary and meaningless division into clubs by organizations after the manner of English colleges which shall represent something definite in the general life of the university.

III

A LITTLE SCRIMMAGE WITH ENGLISH RUGBY

THE relationship between the colleges and the university exists in a greater or less degree in all sports. There is a series of matches among the leading colleges in cricket, and a " cup tie " in Association football. These sports are almost as popular as rowing, and have many excellences which it would be pleasant to point out and profitable perhaps to emulate; but it seems best to concentrate attention on the sports which are best understood in America, such as Rugby football and athletics. The workings of the college system may be most clearly seen in them, and the spirit of English sportsmanship most sympathetically appreciated.

The rivalry between the Association and the Rugby games has made English football players quite unexpectedly sensitive to comparisons. I had scarcely set foot upon a Rugby field when I was confronted with the inevitable question as to English Rugby and American. I replied that from a hasty judgment the English game seemed haphazard and inconsequent. "We don't kill one another, if that's what you mean by 'inconsequent,'" my companion replied; and I soon found that a report that two players had been killed in the Thanksgiving Day match of the year before had never been contradicted in England. "That is the sport," my friend continued, "which Caspar Whitney says, in his 'Sporting Pilgrimage,' has improved English Rugby off the face of the earth!"

The many striking differences between English and American Rugby arise out of the features of our game known as "possession of the ball" and "interference." In the early days of the American game, many of the most sacred English traditions were unknown, and the wording of the English rules proved in practice so far from explicit that it was not possible to discover what it meant, much less to enforce the rules.

One of the traditions favored a certain comparative mildness of demeanor. The American players, on the contrary, favored a campaign of personal assault for which the general rules of the English scrummage lent marked facilities. It soon became necessary in America to line the men up in loose order facing each other, and to forbid violent personal contact until the actual running with the ball should begin. This clearly made it necessary that the sides should in turn put the ball in play, and consequently should alternately have possession of it. Under this arrangement, each side is in turn organized on the offensive and the defensive.

The upshot of this was that the forwards, who in the parent English game have only an incidental connection with the running of the backs, become a part of each successive play, opening up the way for the progress of the ball. According to the English code, this made our forwards off-side, so that the rule had to be changed to fit the new practice. It then appeared that if the forwards could play ahead of the ball, the backs could do so too; and here you have the second great American feature. The result of " possession " of the ball and " interference " is an elaborate and almost military code of tactics unknown in the English game.

In the course of time I had unusual facilities for observing English Rugby. During the Morrison wine which ended the season of tubbing on the river, the captain of the Balliol fifteen threw his arms about me, and besought me to play on the team. He had not a single three-quarters, he said, who could get out of his own way running. I pleaded an attack of rheumatism and ignorance of the game. He said it did not matter. "And I'm half blind,' I added. "So am I," he interrupted, "but we'll both be all right in the morning." I said I referred to the fact that I was very near-sighted; but he took all excuses as a sign of re-sentment because he had failed to invite me to breakfast in my freshman term; he appeared to think it his duty to breakfast all possible candi-dates. Such are the courtesies of an English cap-tain, and such are the informalities of English training.

The next morning the captain wrote me that there was a match on against Merton, and asked me to come out a quarter of an hour before the rest for a little coaching. A quarter of an hour to learn to play football! In spite of the captain's predictions of the night before, I was not so sure that he was yet "all right;" so I went out to the porter's lodge and scanned the bulletin board. My name stared me in the face. I had scarcely time to take luncheon and don a pair of football shorts.

The practice my coach gave me consisted in run-ning the length of the field three or four times, passing the ball back and forth as we went. His instructions with regard to the game were equally simple. To keep in proper position I had only to watch my Merton *vis-à-vis* and take a place symmetrical with his. When the enemy heeled the ball out of the " scrummage " to their quarter-back, putting us for the moment on the defensive, I was to watch my man, and, if the ball was passed to him, to tackle him. If he passed it before I could tackle him I was still to follow him, leaving the man who took the ball to be watched by my neighbor, in order that I might be on hand if my man received it again. An American back, when his side is on the defensive, is expected to keep his eye on his *vis-à-vis* while the ball is being snapped back ; but his main duty is to follow the ball. An English back under similar circumstances is expected only to follow his man. If our side happened to heel out the ball from the scrum and one of our three-quarters began to run with it, we were on the offensive, and the other three-quarters and I were to follow at his heels, so that when he was about to be tackled — " collared," the English say — he could pass it on to us. There is, as I have said, no such thing as combined " interference " among the backs. A player who gets between the man with the ball and the enemy's goal is rankly off-side. It is not to be understood that the captain coached all this information into me. I had to buttonhole him and pump it out word by word. Coaching of any sort is all but unknown on Eng-

AN ENGLISH RUGBY LINE-UP

To the left of the scrum, two half backs and six three-quarter backs face each other in pairs

lish football fields. What there is of the game is learned at school — or in the nursery!

When the opposing teams scattered over the field for the kick-off, I noticed with satisfaction that there was not a spectator on the grounds to embarrass me. It is so in almost all English college games — the fellows are more than likely to have sports of their own on, and anyway, what is the use in hanging round the fields where other fellows are having all the fun?

On the kick-off, luckily, the ball did not come to my corner of the field, for I could scarcely have seen it, much less caught it. Our side returned the kick and the "scrum" formed. The nine forwards gathered compactly in a semi-ellipse, bent their bodies together in a horizontal plane, with their heads carefully tucked beneath the mass, and leaned against the opposing mass of forwards, who were similarly placed. When the two scrums were thoroughly compacted, the umpire tossed the ball on the ground beneath the opposing sets of legs, whereupon both sides began to struggle. The scrum in action looks like a huge tortoise with a score of legs at each end, which by some unaccountable freak of nature are struggling to walk in opposite directions. The sight is certainly awe-inspiring, and it was several days before I realized that it masked no abstrusely working tactics; there is little, if anything, in it beyond the obvious grunting and shoving.

The backs faced each other in pairs ranged out on the side of the scrum that afforded the broader field for running. The legs in the Balliol scrum pushed harder and the bodies squirmed to more advantage, for our men had presently got the ball among their feet. They failed to hold it there, however, and it popped out into a half-back's hands. He passed it quickly to one of my companions at three-quarters, who dodged his man and ran toward the corner of the field. I followed, and just as the full-back collared him he passed the ball to me. Before I had taken three rheumatic strides I had two men hanging at my back; but when they brought me down, the ball was just beyond the line. The audience arose as one man — to wit, the referee, who had been squatting on the side lines — and shouted, " Played. Well played!" I had achieved universal fame. During the rest of the game the Balliol scrum, which was a very respectable affair of its kind, kept the ball to itself, while we backs cooled our heels.

A few days later, in a game against Jesus, the scrums were more evenly matched, and the ball was heeled out oftener. I soon found that my eyes were not sharp enough to follow quick passing; and when, just before half-time, a punt came in my direction, I was horrified to see the ball multiply until it looked like a flock of balloons. As luck had it, I singled out the wrong balloon to catch. Jesus fell on the ball just as it bounced over the goal-line. In the second half the captain put one of the forwards in my place, and put me in the scrum.

The play here was more lively, though scarcely more complex or difficult. Each forward stuck his head beneath the shoulders of the two men in front of him, grasped their waists, and then heaved, until, when the ball popped out of the scrum, the word came to dissolve. There were absolutely no regular positions; the man who was in the front centre of one scrummage might be in the outskirts of the next. On some teams, I found, by inquiry, a definite order is agreed on, but this is regarded as of doubtful advantage.

When the umpire or a half-back tosses the ball into the scrummage, there are, at an ultimate analysis, four things that can happen. First, the two sides may struggle back and forth, carrying the ball on the ground at their feet; this play is called a " pack." Second, the stronger side may cleave the weaker, and run down the field, dribbling the ball yard by yard as they go, until either side picks it up for a run, or else drops on it and cries " down." Third, one side may be able to " screw the scrum," a manœuvre which almost rises to the altitude of a " play."   The captain shouts " Right! " or perhaps " Left! " and then his forwards push diagonally, instead of directly, against their opponents. The result is very like what we used to call a revolving wedge, except that, since the ball is carried on the ground, the play eventuates, when successful, in a scattering rush of forwards down the field, dribbling the ball at their feet, just as when the scrum has been cloven.   The fourth possibility is that the side that gets the ball amongst its eighteen legs allows it to ooze out behind, or, if its backs are worthy of confidence, purposely heels it out.   Thereupon results the play I have already described : one of the half-backs pounces upon it and passes it deftly to the three-quarters, who run with it down the field, if necessary passing it back and forth.   In plays which involve passing or dribbling, English teams sometimes reach a very high degree of skill : few sights on the football field are more inspiring than to see a " combination " of players rush in open formation among their opponents, shifting the ball from one to another with such rapidity and accuracy as to elude all

THROWING IN THE BALL

attempts to arrest it. As a whole, the game of the forwards is much more fun than that of the backs, though decidedly less attractive in the eyes of the spectators — a consideration of slight importance on an English field!

Just as I began to get warmed to my new work I smashed my nose against the head of a Balliol man who was dodging back into the push. The captain told me that I need not finish the game; but as it is against the English rules to substitute players and we were still far from sure of winning, I kept to my grunting and shoving. At the end of the game the captain very politely gave me the hoof. This was just what I expected and deserved; but I was surprised to find that the fellows had objected to my playing the game through with a bloody nose. They would have preferred not to be bled upon.

This regard for pleasantness and convenience, which to an American is odd enough, is characteristic even of 'varsity football. The slenderness of the preliminary training of a 'varsity fifteen is incredible to any American who has not witnessed it. To sift the candidates there is a freshman match and a senior match, with perhaps one or two " squashes " — that is to say, informal games — besides. And even these tests are largely a matter of form. Men are selected chiefly on their public school reputations or in consequence of good work on a college fifteen. The process of developing players, so familiar to us, is unknown. There is no coaching of any kind, as we understand the word. When a man has learned the game at his public school or in his college, he has learned it for all time, though he will, of course, improve by playing for the university. The need of concentrated practice is greatly lessened by the fact that the soft English winter allows as long a season of play as is desired. The team plays a game or two a week against the great club teams of England — Blackheath, Richmond, London Scottish, Cardiff, Newport, and Huddersfield — with perhaps a bit of informal kicking and punting between times. When the weather is too bad, it lays off entirely.

All this does not conduce to the strenuousness of spirit Americans throw into their sports. In an inter-varsity match I saw the Oxford team which was fifty per cent. better allow itself to be shoved all over the field : it kept the game a tie only by the rarest good fortune. It transpired later that the gayeties of Brighton, whither the team had gone to put the finishing touches on its training, had been too much for it. In an American uni-

versity such laxity would be thought the lowest
depth of unmanliness, but I could not see that any
one at Oxford really resented it; at most it was a
subject for mild sarcasm. You can't expect a team
to be in the push everywhere !

This lack of thorough preparation is even more
characteristic of the international teams — England, Ireland, Scotland, and Wales — that yearly
play for the championship of Great Britain. They
are chosen from the most brilliant players in the
leading clubs, and local jealousy makes the task of
choosing most delicate. The temptation is to take
a man or two impartially from each of the great
fifteens. As the international teams take little or
no practice as a whole, the tendency in the great
games is to neglect the finer arts of dribbling and
passing in combination — the arts for which each
player was severally chosen — and revert to the
primitive grunting and shoving. In the great
games, accordingly, the team which is man for man
inferior as regards the fine points may prevail by
sheer strength, so that the result is liable to be
most unsatisfactory. Some years ago, owing to
local jealousy, the Welsh international had to be
chosen mainly from a single club — with the result
that it won the championship; and in 1901 the
canny Scotch team won by intentionally selecting

its members, in spite of local jealousy, on the score of their familiarity with one another's play.

The very rules under which the game is played are calculated to moderate the struggle. As a result of the rule against substituting, to which I have referred, any extreme of hard play in · the practice games, such as lays off dozens of good American players yearly, is not likely to be encouraged. Of course good men " crock," as they call it ; but where an injury is practically certain to disqualify a man from the inter-varsity match, the football limp and the football patch can scarcely be regarded as the final grace of athletic manhood. Willful brutality is all but unknown ; the seriousness of being disqualified abets the normal English inclination to play the game like a person of sense and good feeling. The physical effect of the sport is to make men erect, lithe, and sound. And the effect on the nervous system is similar. The worried, drawn features of the American player on the eve of a great contest are unknown. An Englishman could not understand how it has happened that American players have been given sulphonal during the last nights of training. English Rugby is first of all a sport, an exercise that brings manly powers into play ; as Hamlet would say, the play 's the thing. It is eminently an enjoyable pastime, pleasant to watch, and more pleasant to take part in.

That our American game is past hoping for on the score of playability is by no means certain. As the historical critics of literature are fond of saying, a period of rapid development is always marked by flagrant excesses, and the development of modern American football has been of astonishing rapidity. Quite often the game of one season has been radically different from the games of all preceding seasons. This cannot continue always, for the number of possible variations is obviously limited, and when the limit is reached American Rugby will be, like English Rugby, the same old game year in and year out. Everybody, from the youngest prep. to the oldest grad., will know it and love it.

The two vital points in which our game differs from the English — " possession of the ball " and " interference " — are both the occasion of vigorous handling of one's opponents. When an American player is tackled, he seldom dares to pass the ball for fear of losing possession of it, so that our rule is to tackle low and hard, in order to stop the ball sharply, and if possible to jar it out of the runner's grasp. In England, it is still fair play to grab a man by the ankle. This is partly because of the softness of the moist thick English turf; but more largely because, as passing is the rule, the tackler in nine cases out of ten aims at the ball. The result is that a man is seldom slammed to the earth as he would be in our game. It is this fact that enables the English player to go bare-kneed.

The danger from interference in the American game is also considerable. When a man is blocked off, he is liable to be thrown violently upon the far from tender bosom of our November mother-earth. Any one familiar with the practice of an American eleven will remember the constant cry of the coaches: "Knock your man on the ground! Put him out of the play!" It has been truly enough said that the American game has exaggerated the most dangerous features of the two English games — the tackling of English Rugby and the " charging" or body-checking of the Association game.

Yet this is only a partial statement of the case. These elements of possession of the ball and interference have raised our game incalculably above the English game as a martial contest. Whereas English Rugby has as yet advanced very little beyond its first principles of grunting and shoving, the American game has always been supreme as a school and a test of courage; and it has always tended, albeit with some excesses, toward an incomparably high degree of skill and strategy. Since American football is still in a state of transitiou, it is only fair to judge the two games by the norm to which they are severally tending. The Englishman has on the whole subordinated the elements of skill in combination to the pleasantness of the sport, while the American has somewhat sacrificed the playability of the game to his insatiate struggle for success and his inexhaustible ingenuity in achieving it. More than any other sport, Rugby football indicates the divergent lines along which the two nations are developing. By preferring either game a man expresses his preference for one side of the Atlantic over the other.

IV

TRACK AND FIELD ATHLETICS

IN track and field athletics, the pleasantness and informality of English methods of training reach a climax. In America we place the welfare of our teams in the hands of a professional trainer, who, through his aide-de-camp, the undergraduate captain, is apt to make the pursuit of victory pretty much a business. Every autumn newcomers are publicly informed that it is their duty to the university to train for the freshman scratch games. At Oxford, I was surprised to find, there was not only no call for candidates, but no trainer to whom to apply for aid. The nearest approach to it was the groundsman at the Iffley Running Grounds, a retired professional who stoked the boilers for the baths, rolled the cinder-path, and occasionally acted as "starter." As his "professional" reputation as a trainer was not at stake in the fortunes of the Oxford team, his attitude was humbly advisory. The president of the Athletic Club never came near the grounds, being busy with rowing on a 'varsity trial eight, and later with playing Association football for the university. To one accustomed to train not only for the glory of his alma mater but for the reputation of his trainer, the situation was uninspiring.

As I might have expected, the impetus to train came from the college. I was rescued from a fit of depression by a college-mate, a German, who wanted some one to train with. At school he had run three miles in remarkable time; but later, when an officer in the German army, his horse had rolled over him at the finish of a steeple-chase, and the accident had knocked out his heart; so he was going to try to sprint. I advised him against all training, and the groundsman shook his head. Yet he was set upon showing the Englishmen in Balliol that a German could be a sportsman. This was no idle talk, as I found later, when he fainted in the bath after a fast hundred, and failed by no one knows how little of coming to. We were soon joined by a third Balliol man, a young Greek poet, whose name is familiar to all who are abreast of the latest literary movement at Athens. He was taking up with athletics because of his interest in the revival of the ancient glories of Greece. When I asked him what distance suited him best — whether he was a sprinter or a runner — he answered with the sweet reasonableness of the Hel-

133

lenic nature that any distance would suit him that
suited me. A motlier trio than we, I suppose,
never scratched a cinder-path. Yet the fellows in
our college seemed almost as interested as they
were amused; and we soon found that even so
learned a place as Balliol would have been glad
to bolster its self-esteem by furnishing its quota
of "running blues." What was lacking in the
way of stimulus from the university was more
than made up for by the spontaneous interest of
the fellows in college.

The rudimentary form of athletics is in meetings held by the separate colleges. These occur
throughout the athletic season, namely, the autumn
term and the winter term; and as hard on to a
score of colleges give them, they come off pretty
often. The prizes are sums of money placed with
the Oxford jeweler, to be spent in his shop as the
winners see fit. In America, the four classes, which
are the only sources of athletic life independent
of the university, are so moribund socially that it
never occurs to them to get out on the track for
a day's sport. It is true that we sometimes hold
inter-class games, but the management of these is
in the hands of the university; they are inspired
solely by a very conscious attempt to develop new
men, and to furnish the old ones with practice in

racing. The vitality of the athletic spirits in the English colleges is witnessed by the fact that an Oxford college frequently meets a fit rival at Cambridge in a set of dual games just for the fun of it.

The only bond between the numerous college meetings and the university sports is a single event in each, called a strangers' race, which is open to all comers. The purpose of these races is precisely that of our inter-class meetings — to give all promising athletes practice in competition. As the two prizes in each strangers' race average five pounds and thirty shillings respectively, the races are pretty efficient. Though the " blues" sometimes compete — Cross made his record of 1 m. $54\frac{2}{5}$s. for the half mile in one of them — they generally abandon them to the new men of promise. While the president and the " blues" generally are rowing and playing football, the colleges thus automatically develop new material for the team.

The climax of the athletic meetings of the autumn term is the freshman sports, held on two days, with a day's interval. The friends of the various contestants make up a far larger audience than one finds at similar sports in America; and a brass band plays while the races are on. The whole thing is decidedly inspiring; and for the first time one is brought face to face with the fact that there are inter-varsity games in store.

When the winter term opens, bleak and rainy, the strangers' races bring out more upper class-men. By and by the " blues " themselves appear in sweater, muffler, and blazer, and " paddle " about the track to supple their muscles and regain disused racing strides. At the end of a fortnight I noticed a middle-aged gentleman with whom the prominent athletes conferred before and after each day's work. I soon found that he was Mr. C. N. Jackson, a don of Hertford College, who should always be remembered as the first hurdler to finish in even time. It is he who — save the mark — takes the place of our American trainers. At one of our large American universities about this time, as I afterwards learned, a very different scene was enacting. The trainer and the captain called a mass-meeting and collected a band of Mott Haven champions of the past to exhort the University to struggle free from athletic disgrace. Though the inter-varsity games were nearly four months in the future — instead of six or seven weeks as at Oxford — those ancient athletes aroused such enthusiasm that 268 men undertook the three months of indoor training. To one used to such exhortations, the Oxford indifference was as chilling as the weather we were all training in. Mr. Jackson seemed never to notice me; and how could I address him when he had not even asked me to save the university from disgrace? I was forced to the unheroic expedient of presenting a card of introduction. To my surprise, I found that he had been carefully watching my work from day to day, but had not felt justified in giving advice until I asked for it.

Even during the final period of training, everything happened so pleasantly and naturally that I had none of the nervous qualms common among American athletes. At first I thought I missed the early morning walks our teams take daily, the companionship and jollity of the training-table, and the sense that the team was making a common sacrifice for an important end. Yet here, too, the college made up in a large measure for what I failed to find in the university. One of our eightsmen was training with a scrub four that was to row a crew of schoolboys at Winchester; and we had a little course of training of our own. Every morning we walked out for our dip to Parson's Pleasure, and breakfasted afterward beneath an ancient ivied window in the common room. In the pleasantness and quiet of those sunlit mornings, I began to realize that our training-table mirth, which is sometimes so boisterous, is in part at least due to intense excitement and overwrought nerves. And the notion of self-sacrifice, which appeals to us so deeply, seemed absurd where we were all training for the pleasure and wholesomeness of sport, and for the sake of a ribbon of blue.

The interest the university took in our welfare became made manifest when the "first strings" were sent off to Brighton for the change in climate which all English teams require before great games. Some of the rest of us, who had nowhere else to go, went with them, but most of the men went home to train. The second string in the three miles stayed up at Oxford for commemoration, and joined us after three consecutive nights of dancing. He said that he found he needed staying up work.

Every morning at Brighton the president made the round of our quarter of the hotel shortly before eight o'clock, and spoiled our waking naps to rout us out for our morning's walk, which included a plunge into the Channel. For breakfast, as indeed for all our meals, we had ordinary English fare, with the difference only that it was more abundant.

On alternate days our training consisted in cross-country walks of ten or a dozen miles. Our favorite paths led along the chalk cliffs, and commanded a lordly view of the Channel. Sometimes, for the sake of variety, we went by train to the Devil's Dyke and tramped back over the downs, now crossing golf-links and now skirting cornfields ablaze with poppies. All this walking filled our lungs with the Brighton air, and by keeping our minds off our races, prevented worry. Sprinters and distance men walked together, though the sprinters usually turned back a mile or two before the rest. The rate prescribed was three and a half miles an hour; but our spirits rose so high that we had trouble in keeping it below five.[1]

The training dinners furnished the really memorable hours of the day. A half-pint of " Burton bitter " was a necessity, and a pint merely rations. If one preferred, he might drink Burgundy *ad lib.*, or Scotch and soda. After trials there was champagne. When I told the fellows that in America our relaxation consists in ice-cream for Sunday dinner, they set me down as a humorist. After dinner, instead of coffee and tobacco, we used to go out to the West Pier, which was a miniature Coney Island, and amuse ourselves with the various attractions. The favorite diversion was seeing the Beautiful Living Lady Cremated. The attraction was the showman, who used to give an elabo-

1 For a note on the value of walking as a part of athletic training, see Appendix I.

rate oration in Lancashire brogue. Every word
of it was funny, but especially the closing sentence:
"The Greeks 'ad a ancient custom of porun' a lie-
bation on the cinders of the departud, which custom, gentlemen, we omits." We used to laugh so
heartily at this that the showman would join in,
and even the beautiful living lady would snicker
companionably, as she crawled away beneath the
stage. If the reader is unable to see the fun of
it, there is no help for him — except, perhaps,
an English training dinner.

The rest of the evenings we used to spend in
strolling about among the crowd, breathing the
salt air, and listening to the music. We did not
lack companionship, for the Oxford and Cambridge
cricket elevens were at Brighton, and the entire
Cambridge athletic team. Many of the cricketers,
and not a few of the Cambridge athletes — whom
the Oxford men called "Cantabs," and sometimes
even "Tabs" — paraded the place puffing bulldog
pipes. The outward relationship between the rival
teams was simply that of man to man. If one
knew a Cambridge man he joined him, and intro-
duced the fellows he happened to be walking with.
One day the Cambridge president talked frankly
about training, urging us to take long walks, and
inviting us to go with his men. The only reason

we did not go was that our day for walking happened to be different from theirs.

The days on which we did our track work we spent largely in London, at the Queen's Club grounds, in order to get a general sense of the track and of the conditions under which the sports were to take place. Sometimes, however, we ran at Preston Park, on the outskirts of Brighton.

On the day of the inter-varsity meeting, our team came together as a whole for the first time in the dressing-rooms of the Queen's Club. The fellows dropped in one by one, in frock coats, top hats, and with a general holiday air. The Oxford broad-jumper, who was the best man at the event in England, had been so busy playing cricket all season, and smoking his pipe with the other cricketers on the pier at Brighton, that he had not had time even to send to Oxford for his jumping-shoes. In borrowing a pair he explained that unless a fellow undertook the fag of thorough training, he could jump better without any practice. Our weight-thrower, a freshman, had surprised himself two days previously by making better puts than either of the Cambridge men had ever done; but as nobody had ever thought it worth while to coach him, he did not know how he had done it, and was naturally afraid he could n't do it again. He showed that he was a freshman by appearing to care whether or not he did his best; but even his imagination failed to grasp the fact that the team which won was to have the privilege of meeting Yale in America. As it turned out, if either of these men had taken his event, Oxford, instead of Cambridge, would have met Yale.

As I went out to start in my race, the question of half-sleeves which Englishmen require in all athletic contests was settled in my mind. The numberless seasonable gowns in the stands and the innumerable top hats ranged on all sides about the course made me feel as if I were at a lawn party rather than at an athletic meeting. I suffered as a girl suffers at her first evening party, or rather as one suffers in those terrible dreams where one faces the problem of maintaining his dignity in company while clad in a smile or so. Waiving the question of half-sleeves, I should have consented to run in pyjamas.

In the race I had an experience which raised a question or two that still offer food for reflection. As my best distance — a half mile — was not included in the inter-varsity program, I ran in the mile as second string. There was a strong wind and the pace was pretty hot, even for the best of us, namely, the Cambridge first string, who had won

the race the year before in 4 min. 19$\frac{4}{5}$ sec., —
the fastest mile ever run in university games. As
the English score in athletic games, only first places
count, and on the second of the three laps I found
myself debating whether it is not unnecessarily
strenuous to force a desperate finish where the
only question is how far a man can keep in front
of the tail end. Several of the fellows had already
dropped out in the quietest and most matter of
fact manner; and as we were finishing the lap
against the wind, I became a convert to the English code of sportsmanship.

As the bunch drew away from me and turned
into the easy going of the sheltered stretch, I was
filled with envy of them, and with uncontrollable
disgust at myself, the like of which I had never
felt when beaten, however badly, after making a
fair struggle. And when I saw them finishing
against the hurricane, striding as if they were running upstairs, I felt the heroism of a desperate
finish as I had never done before. It did not help
matters when I realized that it was the last race I
was ever to run.

At the Sports' dinner that night at the Holborn
Restaurant, I pocketed some of my disgust. The
occasion was so happy that I remember wishing
we might have something like it after our meet-

ings at home, for good-fellowship chastens the pride of winning and gives dignity to honest defeat. There was homage for the victors and humorous sympathy for the vanquished. Light blue and dark blue applauded and poked fun at each other impartially. Sir Richard Webster, Q. C., now Lord Chief Justice, himself an old blue, presided at the dinner, and explained how it was that the performances of his day were really not to be sneezed at; and the young blues, receiving their prizes, looked happy and said nothing. After dinner, we divided into squads and went to the Empire Theatre of Varieties, Cantab locking arms with Oxonian. By supper time, at St. James', I was almost cheerful again.

Yet the disgust of having quitted that race has never left me. The spirit of English sportsmanship will always seem to me very gracious and charming. As a nation, I think we can never be too thankful for the lesson our kinspeople have to teach us in sportsmanly moderation and in chivalry toward an opponent. But every man must draw his own line between the amenities of life and the austerities; and I know one American who hopes never again to quit a contest, even a contest in sport, until he has had the humble satisfaction of doing his best.

ENGLISH AND AMERICAN SPORTSMANSHIP

THE prevalence of out-of-door sports in England, and the amenity of the English sporting spirit, may be laid, I think, primarily, to the influence of climate. Through the long, temperate summer, all nature conspires to entice a man out of doors, while in America sunstroke is imminent. All day long the village greens in England are thronged with boys playing cricket in many-colored blazers, while every stream is dotted with boats of all sorts and descriptions; and in the evenings, long after the quick American twilight has shut down on the heated earth, the English horizon gives light for the recreations of those who have labored all day. In the winter the result is the same, though the cause is very different. Stupefying exhalations rise from the damp earth, and the livelong twilight that does for day forces a man back for good cheer upon mere animal spirits. In the English summer no normal man could resist the beckoning of the fields and the river. In the winter it is sweat, man, or die.

It is perhaps because of the incessant call to be out of doors that Englishmen care so little to have their houses properly tempered. At my first dinner with the dons of my college, the company assembled about a huge sea-coal fire. On a rough calculation the coal it consumed, if used in one of our steam-heaters, would have heated the entire college to incandescence. As it was, its only effect seemed to be to draw an icy blast across our ankles from mediæval doors and windows that swept the fire bodily up the chimney, and left us shivering. One of the dons explained that an open fire has two supreme advantages: it is the most cheerful thing in life, and it insures thorough ventilation. I agreed with him heartily, warming one ankle in my palms, but demurred that in an American winter heat was as necessary as cheerfulness and ventilation. "But if one wears thick woolens," he replied, " the cold and draught are quite endurable. When you get too cold reading, put on your great-coat." I asked him what he did when he went out of doors. "I take off my great-coat. It is much warmer there, especially if one walks briskly." Some days later, when I went to dine with my tutor, my hostess apologized for the chill of the drawing-room. "It will presently be much warmer," she added; "I have always noticed that when you have sat in a room awhile, it gets warm from the heat of your bodies." She proved to be right. But when we went into the dining-room, we found it like a barn. She smiled with repeated reassurances. Again she proved right; but we had hardly tempered the frost when we had to shift again to the drawing-room, which by this time again required, so to speak, to be acclimated. Meanwhile my tutor, who was of a jocular turn of mind, diverted our thoughts from our suffering by ragging me about American steam heat, and forced me, to his infinite delight, to admit that we aim to keep our rooms warmed to sixty-eight degrees Fahrenheit. Needless to say, this don was an athlete. As the winter wore away, I repeatedly saw him in Balliol hockey squashes, chasing the ball about with the agility of a terrier pup. At nightfall, no doubt, he returned to his wife and family prepared to heat any room in the house to the required temperature. Heaven forbid that I should resent the opprobrium Englishmen heap upon our steam heat! I merely wish to point out that the English have failed as signally as we, though for the opposite reason, in making their houses habitable in the winter, and that an Englishman is forced into athletics to resist the deadly stupefaction of a Bœotian climate, and to keep his house warm.

AN AMERICAN AT OXFORD

In a sportsman it would be most ungracious to inveigh against English weather. The very qualities one instinctively curses make possible the full and varied development of outdoor games, which Americans admire without stint. Our football teams do day labor to get fit, and then, after a game or so, the sport is nipped in the bud. To teach our oarsmen the rudiments of the stroke we resort to months of the galley-slavery of tank-rowing. Our track athletes begin their season in the dead of winter with the dreary monotony of wooden dumb-bells and pulley-weights, while the baseball men are learning to slide for bases in the cage. In England the gymnasium is happily unknown. Winter and summer alike the sportsman lives beneath the skies, and the sports are so diverse and so widely cultivated that any man, whatever his mental or physical capacity, finds suitable exercise that is also recreation.

It is because of this universality of athletic sports that English training is briefer and less severe. The American makes, and is forced to make, a long and tedious business of getting fit, whereas an Englishman has merely to exercise and sleep a trifle more than usual, and this only for a brief period. Our oarsmen work daily from January to July, about six months, or did so before Mr. Lehmann brought English ideas among us; the English 'varsity crews row together nine or ten weeks. Our football players slog daily for six or seven weeks; English teams seldom or never " practice," and play at most two matches a week. Our track athletes are in training at frequent intervals throughout the college year, and are often at the training-table six weeks; in England six weeks is the maximum period of training, and the men as a rule are given only three days a week of exercise on the cinder-track. To an American training is an abnormal condition; to an Englishman it is the consummation of the normal.

The moderation of English training is powerfully abetted by a peculiarity of the climate. The very dullness and depression that make exercise imperative also make it impossible to sustain much of it. The clear, bright American sky — the sky that renders it difficult for us to take the same delight in Italy as an Englishman takes, and leads us to prefer Ruskin's descriptions to the reality — cheers the American athlete; and the crispness of the atmosphere and its extreme variability keeps his nerves alert. An English athlete would go hopelessly stale on work that would scarcely key an American up to his highest pitch.

The effect of these differences on the temperament of the athlete is marked. The crispness and variety of our climate foster nervous vitality at the expense of physical vitality, while the equability of the English climate has the opposite effect. In all contests that require sustained effort — distance running and cross-country running, for example — we are in general far behind; while during the comparatively few years in which we have practiced athletic sports we have shown, on the whole, vastly superior form in all contests depending upon nervous energy — sprinting, hurdling, jumping, and weight-throwing.

Because of these differences of climate and of temperament, no rigid comparisons can be made between English and American training; but it is probably true that English athletes tend to train too little. Mr. Horan, the president of the Cambridge team that ran against Yale at New Haven, said as much after a very careful study of American methods; but he was not convinced that our thoroughness is quite worth while. The law of diminishing returns, he said, applies to training as to other things, so that, after a certain point, very little is gained even for a great sacrifice of convenience and pleasantness. Our American athletes are twice as rigid in denying the spirit for an advantage, Mr. Horan admitted, of enough to win by.

The remark is worth recording: it strikes the note of difference between English and American sportsmanship. After making all allowances for the conditions here and abroad that are merely accidental, one vital difference remains. For better or for worse, a sport is a sport to an Englishman, and whatever tends to make it anything else is not encouraged; as far as possible it is made pleasant, socially and physically. Contests are arranged without what American undergraduates call diplomacy; and they come off without jockeying. It is very seldom that an Englishman forgets that he is a man first and an athlete afterwards. Yet admirable as this quality is, it has its defects, at least to the transatlantic mind. Even more, perhaps, than others, Englishmen relish the joy of eating their hearts at the end of a contest, but they have no taste for the careful preparation that alone enables a man to fight out a finish to the best advantage. It is no doubt true, as the Duke of Wellington said, that the battle of Waterloo was won on the playing-fields of England; but for any inconsiderable sum I would agree to furnish a similar saying as to why the generals in South Africa ran into ambush after ambush.

151

In America, sportsmanship is almost a religion. Fellows mortify the flesh for months and leave no means untried that may help to bring honor to their college; or if they don't, public opinion brings swift and sure retribution. It is true that this leads to excesses. Rivalries are so strong that undergraduates have been known to be more than politic in arranging matches with each other. So the graduate steps in to moderate the ardor of emulation, and often ends by keeping alive ancient animosities long after they would have been forgotten in the vanishing generations of undergraduates. The Harvard eleven wants to play the usual football game; but it is not allowed to, because a committee of graduates sees fit to snub Yale; the athletic team wants to accept a challenge from Oxford and Cambridge, but it is not allowed to because Pennsylvania, which is not challenged, has a better team, and it is the policy of the university (which has an eye to its graduate schools) to ingratiate sister institutions. In a word, the undergraduates are left to manage their studies while the faculty manages their pastimes.

When a contest is finally on, excesses are rampant. Of occasional brutalities too much has perhaps been said; but more serious errors are unreproved. There is a tradition that it is the duty of all non-athletes to inspire the 'varsity teams by cheering the play from the side lines; and from time to time one reads leading articles in the college papers exhorting men to back the teams. The spectator is thus given an important part in every contest, and after a 'varsity match he is praised or blamed, together with the members of the team, according to his deserts. Yale may outplay Harvard, but if Harvard sufficiently outcheers Yale she wins, and to the rooters belong the praise. In baseball games especially, a season's championship is not infrequently decided by the fact that the partisans of one side are more numerous, or for other reasons make more noise. These are serious excesses, and are worthy of the pen of the robustest reformer; but after all has been said they are incidents, and in the slow course of time are probably disappearing.

The signal fact is that our young men do what they do with the diligence of enthusiasm, and with the devotion that inspires the highest courage. It is not unknown that, in the bitterness of failure, American athletes have burst into tears. When our English cousins hear of this they are apt to smile, and doubtless the practice is not altogether to be commended; but in the length and breadth of a man's experience there are only two or three

153

things one would wish so humbly as the devotion that makes it possible. Such earnestness is the quintessence of Americanism, and is probably to be traced to the signal fact that in the struggle of life we all start with a fighting chance of coming out on top. Whatever the game, so long as it is treated as a game, nothing could be as wholesome as the spirit that tends to make our young men play it for all it is worth, to do everything that can be done to secure victory with personal honor. In later years, when these men stand for the honor of the larger alma mater, on the field of battle or in the routine of administration, it is not likely that they will altogether forget the virtues of their youth.

The superiority of English sportsmanship arises, not from the spirit of the men, but from the breadth of the development of the sports, and this, climate aside, is the result of the division of the university into colleges. The average college of only a hundred and fifty men maintains two football teams — a Rugby fifteen and an Association eleven — an eight and two torpids, a cricket eleven, and a hockey eleven. Each college has also a set of athletic games yearly. If we add the men who play golf, lawn and court tennis, rackets and fives, who swim, box, wrestle, and who shoot on the

154

ranges of the gun club, the total of men schooled in competition reaches eighty to one hundred. A simple calculation will show that when so many are exercising daily, few are left for spectators. Not a bench is prepared, nor even a plank laid on the spongy English turf, to stand between the hanger-on and pneumonia. A man's place is in the field of strife; to take part in athletic contests is almost as much a matter of course as to bathe. Of late years there has been a tendency in England to believe that the vigor of undergraduates — and of all Englishmen, for the matter of that — is in decadence. As regards their cultivation of sports at least, the reverse is true. Contests are more numerous now than ever, and are probably more earnestly waged. What is called English decadence is in reality the increasing superiority of England's rivals.

Quite aside from the physical and moral benefit to the men engaged, this multiplication of contests has a striking effect in lessening the importance of winning or losing any particular one of them. It is more powerful than any other factor in keeping English sports free from the excesses that have so often characterized our sports. From time to time a voice is raised in America as of a prophet of despair demanding the abolition of inter-university contests. As yet the contests have not been abolished, and do not seem likely to be. Might it not be argued without impertinence that the best means of doing away with the excesses in question is not to have fewer contests, but more of them ? If our universities were divided into residential units, corresponding roughly to the English colleges, the excesses in particular contests could scarcely fail to be mitigated ; and what is perhaps of still higher importance, the great body of non-athletes would be brought directly under the influence of all those strong and fine traditions of undergraduate life which centre in the spirit of sportsmanship.

NOTE. For a discussion of the influences of climate in international athletics, see Appendix II.

III

THE COLLEGE AS AN EDUCATIONAL FORCE

I

THE PASSMAN

IN the educational life of Oxford, as in the social and athletic life, the distinctive feature, at least to the American mind, is the duality of organization in consequence of which an undergraduate is amenable first to his college and then to the university: the college teaches and the university examines. In America, so far as the undergraduate is concerned, the college and the university are identical: the instructor in each course of lectures is also the examiner. It follows from this that whereas in America the degree is awarded on the basis of many separate examinations—one in each of the sixteen or more "courses" which are necessary for the degree — in England it is awarded on the basis of a single examination. For three or four years the college tutor labors with his pupil, and the result of his labors is gauged by an examination, set and judged by the university. This system is characteristic of both Cambridge and Oxford, and for that matter, of all

English education; and the details of its organization present many striking contrasts to American educational methods.

Sir Isaac Newton's happy thought of having a big hole in his door for the cat and a little hole for the kitten must have first been held up to ridicule by an American. In England, the land of classes, it could hardly fail of full sympathy. In America there is but one hole of exit, though men differ in their proportions as they go out through it. In England there are passmen and classmen.

To say that the passman is the kitten would not be altogether precise. He is rather a distinct species of undergraduate. More than that, he is the historic species, tracing his origin quite without break to the primal undergraduate of the Middle Ages. He is a tradition from the time when the fund of liberal knowledge was so small that the university undertook to serve it all up in a pint-pot to whoever might apply. The pint-pot still exists at Oxford; and though the increasing knowledge of nine centuries long ago overflowed its brim, the passman still holds it forth trustfully to his tutor. The tutor patiently mingles in it an elixir compounded of as many educational simples as possible, and then the passman presents it to the examiners, who smile and dub him Bachelor of Arts. After three years, if he is alive and pays the sum of twelve pounds, they dub him Master.

The system for granting the pass degree is, in its broader outlines, the same as for all degrees. In the first examination — that for matriculation — it is identical for passmen and classmen. This examination is called " responsions," and is, like its name, of mediæval origin. It is the equivalent of the American entrance examination; but by one of the many paradoxes of Oxford life it was for centuries required to be taken after the pupil had been admitted into residence in one of the colleges. In the early Middle Ages the lack of preparatory schools made it necessary first to catch your undergraduate. It was not until the nineteenth century that a man could take an equivalent test before coming up, for example at a public school; but it is now fast becoming the rule to do so; and it is probable that all colleges will soon require an entrance examination. In this way two or three terms more of a student's residence are devoted to preparation for the two later and severer university tests.

The subjects required for matriculation are easy enough, according to our standards. Candidates offer : (1) The whole of arithmetic, and either (a) elementary algebra as far as simple equations involving two unknown quantities, or (*b*) the first two books of Euclid ; (2) Greek and Latin grammar, Latin prose composition, and prepared translation from one Greek and one Latin book. The passages for prepared translation are selected from six possible Greek authors and five possible Latin authors. The influence of English colonial expansion is evident in the fact that candidates who are not " European British subjects " may by special permission offer classical Sanskrit, Arabic, or Pali as a substitute for either Greek or Latin : the dark-skinned Orientals, who are so familiar a part of Oxford life, are not denied the right to study the classics of their native tongues. Thus the election of subjects is a well-recognized part of responsions, though the scope of the election does not extend to science and the modern languages.

Once installed in the college and matriculated in the university, both passman and honor man are examined twice and twice only. The first public examination, more familiarly called "moderations," or "mods," takes place in the middle of an undergraduate's course. Here the passmen have only a single subject in common with the men seeking honors, namely, the examination in Holy Scripture, or the Rudiments of Faith and Religion, more familiarly called " Divinners," which is to say Divinities. The subject of the examination is the gospels of St. Luke and St. John in the Greek text; and either the Acts of the Apostles or the two books of Kings in the Revised Version. As in all Oxford examinations, cram-books abound containing a reprint of the questions put in recent examinations; and, as many of these questions recur from year to year, the student of Holy Scripture is advised to master them. A cram-book which came to my notice is entitled " The Undergraduate's Guide to the Rudiments of Faith and Religion," and contains, among other items of useful information: tables of the ten plagues; of the halting-places during the journey in the wilderness; of the twelve apostles; and of the seven deacons. The book recommends that the kings of Judah and Israel, the journeys of St. Paul, and the Thirty-nine Articles shall be committed to memory. The obviously pious author of this guide to the rudiments of these important accomplishments speaks thus cheerfully in his preface : " The compiler feels assured that if candidates will but follow the plan he has suggested, no candidate of even ordinary ability need have the least fear of failure." According to report, it is perhaps not so easy to acquire the rudiments of faith and religion. In a paper set some years ago, as one of

163

the examiners informed me, a new and unexpected question was put: " Name the prophets and discriminate between the major and the minor." One astute passman wrote : " Far be it from me to make discriminations between these wise and holy men. The kings of Judah and Israel are as follows." Unless a man passes the examination, he has to take it again, and the fee to the examiner is one guinea. " This time I go throngh," exclaimed an often ploughed passman. " I need these guineas for cigars." Those who are not " European British subjects " may substitute certain sacred works in Sanskrit, Arabic, or Pali ; and those who object for conscientious scruples to a study of the Bible may substitute the Phædo of Plato ; but the sagacious undergraduate knows that if he does this he must have no conscientious scruples against harder work.

In America there is no such examination, so far as I know. At Harvard an elective course in the history and literature of the Jews is given by the Semitic department ; and if this does not insure success in acquiring the rudiments of faith and religion, it was, on one occasion at least, the means of redoubling the attendance at chapel. Just before the final examination, it transpired that the professor in charge of the course was con-

ducting morning service, and was giving five minute summaries of Jewish history. For ten days
the front pews were crowded with waistcoats of
unwonted brilliance; the so-called sports who had
taken the course as a snap were glad to grind it up
under the very best auspices.

Let me not be misunderstood. In the long run,
the English undergraduates no doubt add greatly
to their chances of spiritual edification. At the
very least they gain a considerable knowledge of
one of the great monuments of the world's literature. In America the Bible is much less read in
families than in England, so that it would seem
much more important to prescribe a course in Biblical history and literature. At one time Professor
Child gave a course in Spenser and the English
Bible, and is said to have been moved at times
when reading before his classes to a truly Elizabethan access of tears. Some years before the
great master died, he gave up the course in despair
at the Biblical ignorance of his pupils. The usual
Harvard undergraduate cannot name five of the
prophets, with or without discrimination, or be certain of five of the kings of Judah. As I write this,
I am painfully uncertain as to whether there were
as many as five.

But to return to our muttons. The remaining

subjects for pass moderations are : (1) Portions of three classic authors, two Greek and one Latin, or two Latin and one Greek. The passages of each author to be studied are prescribed, but the candidate may elect, with certain slight limitations, from eight Greek and eight Latin authors " of the best age." As in the case of responsions and Holy Scripture, Sanskrit, Arabic, or Pali may be substituted for either Greek or Latin. The examination covers not only grammar and literature, but any question arising out of the text. Besides these are required : (2) Latin prose composition ; (3) sight translation of Greek and Latin; and (4) either logic or the elements of geometry and algebra.

The final pass examination allows a considerable range of election. Three general subjects must be offered. At least one of these must be chosen from the following : Greek, Latin, Sanskrit, Persian, German, and French. If a candidate wishes, he may choose two of his three subjects in ancient language, literature, and history, or in modern language, literature, history, and economics. The remaining one or two subjects may be chosen from a dozen courses ranging through the elements of mathemathics, natural science, law, and theology. This range of choice is very different from that in America, in that a student is not permitted freely to elect subjects without reference to one another. For the pass degree, no considerable originality or grasp of the subject is necessary, any more than for an undistinguished degree in an American college; but the body of necessary facts is pretty sure to be well ordered, if not digested. The idea of grouping electives is the fundamental difference between English and American education. In the case of the honor man it will be seen to be of chief importance.

In order to take the Oxford degree, it is further necessary to be in residence three years, and a man may reside four years before going up for his final examination. The period of study — or loafing — may be broken in various ways; and it is characteristic that though a man may anticipate his time and take his last examination before the last term of his third year, he is required to reside at the university, studies or no studies, until the minimum residence is completed. Nothing could indicate more clearly the importance which is attached to the merely social side of university life.

It is, in fact, as a social being that the passman usually shines. You may know him most often from the fact that you sight him in the High by a waistcoat of many colors. At night he is apt to evade the statutes as to academicals; but if he wears his gown, he wraps it about his neck as if it were a muffler, and tilts his mortar-board at all angles. He is the genius of the fox terrier and the bulldog pipe; he rides to the hounds, and is apt in evading the vice-chancellor's regulations as to tandems and four-in-hands. Or perhaps he sits comfortably in his rooms discoursing lightly of the impious philosophies that are the studies of the classman, and writes Horatian verse for the " Isis " and the " Oxford Magazine." He does anything, in fact, that is well-bred, amusing, and not too strenuous. Curiously enough, it sometimes happens that he does sufficient reading on his own account to give him no little real culture. Of late there has been a reaction in favor of the pass school as affording a far better general education.

If the passman loiters through the three or four years, it is mainly the fault — or the virtue — of the public school he comes from. Of late the best public schools have had so strong and admirable an influence that boys have often been kept in them by their parents until they reach the age limit, generally nineteen. By this time they have anticipated most of the studies required for a pass degree in the university, and find little or nothing to do when they go up but to evade their tutors and to " reside." It is by this means, as the satirist long ago explained, that Oxford has become an institution of such great learning. Every freshman brings to it a little knowledge and no graduate takes any away.

There is reason in all this. In the first place, as I have said, the passman is the historical undergraduate, and little short of a convulsion could disestablish him — that is the best of British reasons. Moreover, to be scrupulously just, the passman knows quite as much as the American student who barely takes a degree by cramming a few hours with a venal tutor before each of his many examinations, and perhaps more than the larger proportion of German students who confine their serious interests to the duel and the Kneipe, and never graduate. And then, the Oxonian argues amiably, if it were not for the pass schools, the majority of the passmen would not come to Oxford at all, and would spend their impressionable period in some place of much less amenity. Clearly, they learn all that is necessary for a gentleman to know, and are perhaps kept from a great deal that is dangerous to young fellows with money and leisure. It means much to the aristocracy and nobility of England that, whatever their ambitions and capacities, they are encouraged by the pursuit of a not too elusive A. B. to stay four

169

years in the university. Even the ambitious student profits by the arrangement. Wherever his future may lie, in the public service, in law, medicine, or even the church, it is of advantage to know men of birth and position — of far greater advantage, from the common sensible English point of view, than to have been educated in an atmosphere of studious enthusiasm and exact scholarship.

II

THE HONOR SCHOOLS

THE modern extension of the world's knowledge, with the corresponding advance in educational requirements, which are perhaps the most signal results of the nineteenth century, could not fail to exert a powerful influence on all university teaching. In the United States, the monument to its influence is the elective system. In England, it is the honor schools. Both countries felt the inadequacy of the antique pint-pot of learning. The democratic New World has not dreamed of making a sharp distinction between the indifferent and the ambitious. Under the lead of the scientific spirit of the German universities, it has placed the noblest branches of human knowledge on a par with the least twig of science. With characteristic conservatism England kept the old pint-pot for the unscholarly, to whom its contents are still of value, though extending its scope to suit the changing spirit of the age ; and for those who felt the new ambitions it made new pint-pots, each one of which should contain the essence gathered from a separate field of learning. The new pint-pots are the honor schools, and the children of the new ambition are the honor men.

The honor schools of Oxford are eight in number. Here again the English conservatism is evident. The oldest of them, literæ humaniores, which was at first the only honor school, has for its subject-matter a thorough view of classical language, literature, and thought. It is an *édition de luxe* of the old pass school. Because of the nobjlity of its proportions, it is familiarly called " greats," and it justifies its name by enrolling almost half of all Oxford candidates for the honor degree. An overwhelming majority of famous Oxford graduates have taken their degree in " greats." The other schools are sometimes known as the minor schools. Mathematics was originally a part of the school in literæ humaniores, but was soon made into a separate school. Since then schools have been established in six new subjects — natural science, jurisprudence, modern history, theology, Oriental studies, and English. Under our elective system, a student continues through his four years, choosing each year at random, or as the fates decree, this, that, or the other brief " course." Under the honor system a man decides sooner or later which one of the several branches he most desires, and sets out to master it.

An Oxford man's decision may be made at the outset; but far the larger number of men defer the choice. They do this by reading for moderations, for pass moderations as well as honor mods may be followed by an honor school at finals. The subject-matter for honor mods is, roughly speaking, the same as for pass mods — the classics and kindred studies; but the field covered is considerably more extended, and to take a high class the student is required to exhibit in his examination papers no little grasp of the subjects as a whole, and if possible to develop his own individuality in the process. Having done with moderations, an honor man is forced to choose a final school. The logical sequence of honor mods is literæ humaniores; but one may choose instead modern history, theology, Oriental studies, or English.

The men who commit themselves to a choice at the outset are those who go in for science or jurisprudence. These men begin by reading for a form of moderations known as science preliminaries or jurisprudence preliminaries.

The exact sequence of examinations is fixed only

by common sense. The school of history is open to those who have taken pass mods, and even to those who have taken the jurisprudence preliminary, though mods is usually preferred in order to give a man the use of the necessary languages. If a science man's chief work is to be in astronomy or physics, which require some mathematics, he may take the mathematical mods, and devote only the second half of his course to science.

Even after a man has chosen his subject and begun to work on it with his tutor, there is considerable range of election. As classical mods are supposed to cover all the subjects essential to polite education, election is mainly a question as to the ancient authors read. If a man knows what final school he is to enter, he may choose his authors accordingly. Thus, a history man chooses the ancient historians; a man who intends to enter the school in English literature, the ancient poets and dramatists. In addition to such authors, all candidates for classical mods choose, according to their future needs, one of four subjects : the history of classical literature, comparative classical philology, classical archæology, and logic. The preliminary examinations in natural science and in jurisprudence are concerned with a general view of the field, and thus do not admit of much variation, whatever the branch to be pursued later; and the same is true of mathematical moderations. A man who chooses any one of these three honor schools has made the great choice of bidding good-by to the classics.

In the final schools the range of choice is greater than at moderations, and is greater in some schools than in others. Literæ humaniores offers the least scope for election. The reason is that the subject-matter is a synthetic view of the classic world entire. Still, in so vast a field, a student perforce selects, laying emphasis on those aspects of the ancient world which he considers (or which he expects the examining board to consider) of most interest and importance. It has been objected even at Oxford that such a course of study gives a student little or no training in exact scholarship. The examination statutes accordingly give a choice of one among no less than forty special subjects, the original sources of which a man may thresh out anew in the hope of adding his iota to the field of science; and, on six months' notice, a student may, under approval, select a subject of his own. The unimportance of this part of the "greats" curriculum is evident in the fact that it is recommended, not required.

The history school requires the student to cover

the constitutional and political history of England entire, political science and economy, with economic history, constitutional law, and political and descriptive geography. It also requires a special subject " carefully studied with reference to the original authorities," and a period of general history. If a student does not aim at a first or second class at graduation, he may omit certain parts of all this. In any case, he has to choose from the general history of the modern world one special period for a more detailed examination. In the school of natural science, the student, after filling in the broad outlines of the subject for his preliminary, must choose for his final examination one of the following seven subjects : physics, chemistry, animal physiology, zoölogy, botany, geology, and astronomy. Besides the written examination, a " practical " examination of three hours is required to show the student's ability at laboratory work. These three honor schools are the most important, and may be regarded as representative. After a man has taken one honor degree, for example, in literæ humaniores, he may take another, for example, in modern history. He then becomes a double honor man, and if he has got a first class in both schools, he is a " double first."

In America, the election of studies goes by fragmentary subjects, and the degree is awarded for passing some four such subjects a year, the whole number being as disconnected, even chaotic, as the student pleases or as chance decrees. In England, the degree is granted for final proficiency in a coherent and well-balanced course of study; but within this not unreasonable limit there is the utmost freedom of election. The student first chooses what honor school he shall pursue, and then chooses the general lines along which he shall pursue it.

III

THE TUTOR

IN preparing for his two " public examinations,"
the pupil is solely in the hands of a college
tutor. Any familiar account of the Oxford don is
apt to make him appear to the American, and especially to the German mind, a sufficiently humble
person. His first duty is the very unprofessional
one of making newcomers welcome. He invites
his pupils to breakfast and to dinner, and introduces them to their fellows so that they shall enter
easily into the life of the college; he tells them
to go in for one or another of the various undergraduate activities. As a teacher, moreover, his
position is strikingly similar to that of the venal
tutors in our universities, who amiably keep lame
ducks from halting, and temper the frost of the
examination period to gilded grasshoppers. It is
all this that makes the American scholar so apt to
smile at the tutor, and the German, perhaps, to
sniff. The tutor is not easily put down. If he
replies with anything more than a British silence,
it is to say that after all education cannot be quite

178

dissociated from a man's life among his fellows. And then there is the best of all English reasons why the tutor should think well of his vocation: it is approved by custom and tradition. Newman, Pusey, Jowett, Pater, Stubbs, Lang, and many such were tutors, and they thought it well worth while to spend the better part of each day with their pupils.

Homely as are the primary duties of the tutor, it is none the less necessary that certain information should be imparted. The shadow of the examiners looms across the path twice in the three or four years of an undergraduate's life. There is no dodging it: in order to get a degree, certain papers must be written and well written. Here is where the real dignity of the tutor resides, the attribute that distinguishes him from all German and American teachers. He is responsible to the college that his pupils shall acquit themselves well before the examiners, — that the reputation of the college shall be maintained. By the same token, the examiners are responsible to the university that its degrees shall be justly awarded, so that the course of education in England is a struggle of tutor against examiner. In Germany and in America, an instructor is expected to be a master of his subject; he may be or may not be — and usually is not — a teacher. In England, a tutor may be a scholar, and often is not. His success is measured first and foremost by the excellence of the papers his pupils write. Is Donkin of Balliol a good tutor? Well, rather, he has got more firsts than any don in Oxford; by which is meant of course that his pupils have got the firsts. A college is rated partly by its number of blues and partly by its number of firsts. For a tutor to lead his pupils to success is as sacred a duty as for an athletic undergraduate to play for the university. The leisurely, not to say loafing, tutor of eighteenth-century tradition has been reformed out of existence. If the modern tutor fails of any high attainment as a scholar, it is mainly because he is required to be a very lively, strenuous, and efficient leader of youth.

The means by which the tutor conducts his charges in the narrow path to success in the schools are characteristic. The secret lies in gaining the good-will of the pupil. Thus any breakfasts, luncheons, and dinners that the hospitable tutor gives to his pupils while they are learning the ways of the place are bread cast upon the waters in a very literal sense. For a decent fellow to neglect the just wishes of a teacher to whom he is indebted is easy enough on occasions; but systematically to shirk a genuine debt of gratitude without losing caste with one's self requires supreme ingenuity. If you don't want to get into the clutches of your tutor, don't take the least chance of getting to like him. This is the soundest advice ever given by the wary upper classman. It has not been ordained by nature that the soul of the teacher is sib to the soul of the taught, but clearly, by exercising the humanities, the irrepressible conflict may be kept within bounds.

Sometimes harsher measures are necessary. Then a man is sent up to the Head of the college, which is not at all a promotion. One fellow used to tell a story of how Jowett, the quondam master of Balliol, chastised him. When he reported, the Master was writing, and merely paused to say: "Sit down, Mr. Barnes, you are working with Mr. Donkin, are you not?" The culprit said he was, and sat down. Jowett wrote on, page after page, while the undergraduate fidgeted. Finally Jowett looked up and remarked: "Mr. Donkin says you are not. Good-morning." After that the undergraduate was more inclined to work with Mr. Donkin.

For graver offenses a man is imprisoned within the paradise behind the college walls — "gated," the term is. One fellow I knew — a third year man who roomed out of college — was obliged to lodge in the rooms of the dean, Mr. J. L. Strachan Davidson. The two turned out excellent friends. No one could be altogether objectionable, the undergraduate explained, whose whiskey and tobacco were as good as the dean's. In extreme cases a man may be sent down, but if this happens, he must either have the most unfortunate of dispositions, or the skin of a rhinoceros against tact and kindness.

It is by similar means that the don maintains his intellectual ascendency. Nothing is more foreign to Oxford than an assumption of pedagogic authority. Mr. Hilaire Belloc, who is now not unknown in London as a man of letters, used to tell of a memorable encounter with Jowett. Mr. Belloc was holding forth in his vein of excellent enthusiasm with regard to his countrymen. For a long time Jowett listened with courteously qualified assent, but finally said: "Mr. Belloc, do you know the inscription which is said to stand above the gate to Hell?" Mr. Belloc was ready with the familiar line from Dante. "No, Mr. Belloc, *Ici on parle français.*" The oratory of even a president of the Oxford Union broke down in laughter. Under such a system a mutual confidence increases day by day between teacher and taught, which may end in a comradeship more intimate than that between father and son.)

Our universities are fast adopting the German or pseudo-German idea that an advanced education consists merely in mastering the subject one may choose to pursue. The point of departure is the "course." If we gain the acquaintance of Lowell or Longfellow, Agassiz, Child, or Norton, we have to thank our lucky stars. In England, the social relationship is the basis of the system of instruction.

marvellous thought

agreed

IV

READING FOR EXAMINATIONS

HOW easy is the course of Oxford discipline on the whole is evident in the regulations as to the times for taking the examinations. The earliest date when a man may go up for moderations is his fifth term after matriculation. As there are four terms a year, this earliest date falls at the outset of his second year. For a passman there is apparently no time beyond which it is forbidden to take mods, or finals either. An honor man may repeat his attempts at mods until eight terms are gone — two full and pleasant years; that is, he may take mods in any of three terms — almost an entire year. For finals he may go up as early as his eleventh term, and as late as his sixteenth — giving a latitude of more than a year. If he wishes to take a final examination in a second subject, he may do so up to his twentieth term. Clearly, the pupil's work is done without pressure other than the personal influence of the tutor. When an American student fails to pass his examinations on the hour, he is disclassed and put on

184

probation, the penalty of which is that he cannot play on any of the athletic teams. On this point, at least, the Oxford system of discipline is not the less childish of the two.

As to the nature of the work done, it is aptly expressed in the Oxford term, "reading." The aim is not merely to acquire facts. From week to week the tutor is apt to meet his pupils, and especially the less forward ones, in familiar conversation, often over a cup of tea and a cigarette. He listens to the report of what the pupil has lately been reading, asks questions to see how thoroughly he has comprehended it, and advises him as to what to read next. When there are several pupils present, the conference becomes general, and thus of greater advantage to all. In the discussions that arise, opposing views are balanced, phrases are struck out and fixed in mind, and the sum of the pupil's knowledge is given order and consistency. The best tutors consciously aim at such a result, for it makes all the difference between a brilliant and a dull examination paper, and the examiners highly value this difference.

The staple of tutorial instruction is lectures. In the old days the colleges were mutually exclusive units, each doing the entire work of instruction for its pupils. This arrangement was obviously wasteful, in that it presupposed a complete and adequate teaching force in each of the twenty colleges. Latterly, a system of "intercollegiate lectures" has been devised, under which a tutor lectures only on his best subjects and welcomes pupils from other colleges. These intercollegiate tutorial lectures are quite like lecture courses at an American college, except that they are not used as a means of police regulation. Attendance is not compulsory, and there are no examinations. A man issues from the walls of his college for booty, and comes back with what he thinks he can profit by.

The importance of the university examinations is thus proportionate to their rarity. The examiners are chosen from the best available members of the teaching force of the university; they are paid a very considerable salary, and the term of service is of considerable length. The preparation for the examination, at least as regards honor men, has a significance impossible under our system. Matters of fact are regarded mainly as determining whether a man shall or shall not get his degree; the class he receives — there are four classes — depends on his grasp of facts and upon the aptitude of his way of writing. No man can get either a first or a second class whose knowledge has not been assimilated into his vitals, and who has not attained in some considerable degree the art of expression in language.

One of the incidents of reading is a set of examinations set by the colleges severally. They take place three times a year, at the end of each term, and are called collections — apparently from the fact that at this time certain college fees used to be collected from the students. The papers are set by the dons, and as is the case with all tutorial exercises, the results have nothing at all to do with the class a man receives in the public examinations — mods and finals. I was surprised to find that it was rather the rule to crib; and my inquiries disclosed a very characteristic state of affairs. One man, who was as honorable in all respects as most fellows, related how he had been caught cribbing. His tutor took the crib and examined it carefully. " Quite right," he said. " In fact, excellent. Don't be at any pains to conceal it. By the finals, of course, you will have to carry all these things in your head; at present, all we want to know is how well you can write an examination paper." The emphasis as to the necessity of knowing how to write was quite as genuine as the sarcasm. These examinations have a further interest to Americans. They are probably a debased survival of examinations which in centuries past were a police regulation to test a student's diligence, and thus had some such relation to a degree as our hour examinations, midyears, and finals. In other words, they suggest a future utility for our present midyears and finals, if ever a genuine honor examination is made requisite for an American honor degree.

For the greater part of his course, an undergraduate's reading is by no means portentous. It was Dr. Johnson, if I am not mistaken, whose aim was "five good hours a day." At Oxford, this is the maximum which even a solid reading man requires of himself. During term time most men do much less, for here is another of the endlessly diverting Oxford paradoxes: passman and classman alike aim to do most of their reading in vacations. As usual, a kernel of common sense may be found. If the climate of England is as little favorable to a strenuous intellectual life as it is to strenuous athleticisms, the climate of Oxford is the climate of England to the nth power. A man's intellectual machinery works better at home in the country. And even as the necessity of relaxation is greater at Oxford, so is the chance of having fun and of making good friends — of growing used to the ways of the world of men. The months at the university are the heyday of life. The home friends and the home sports are the same yesterday and forever. The university clearly recognizes all this. It rigidly requires a man to reside at Oxford a certain definite time before graduation; but how and when he studies and is examined, it leaves to his own free choice. A man reads enough at Oxford to keep in the current of tutorial instruction, and to get on the trail of the books to be wrestled with in vacation.

V

THE EXAMINATION

WHEN mods and finals approach, the tune is altered. Weeks and months together the fellows dig and dig, morning, noon, and night. All sport and recreation is now regarded only as sustaining the vital forces for the ordeal. Sometimes, in despair at the distractions of Oxford life, knots of fellow sufferers form reading parties, gain permission to take a house together in the country, and draw up a code of terrible penalties against the man who suggests a turn at whist, the forbidden cup, or a trip to town. From the simplest tutorial cram-book to the profoundest available monograph, no page is left unturned. And this is only half. The motto of Squeers is altered. When a man knows a thing, he goes and writes it. Passages apt for quotation are learned by rote; phrases are polished until they are luminous; periods are premeditated; paragraphs and sections prevised. An apt epigram turns up in talk or in reading — the wary student jots it down, polishes it to a point, and keeps it in ambush to dart it at this or that possible question. One man I knew was electrified with Chaucer's description of the Sergeant of the Law, —

> No wher so bisy a man as he ther nas,
> And yet he semed bisier than he was ; —

and fell into despair because he could not think of any historical personage in his subject-matter to whom it might aptly apply. On the other hand, there was Alfred the Great, whose character was sure to be asked for. Did I know any line of Chaucer that would hit off Alfred the Great? So unusual to quote Chaucer.

All this sort of thing has, of course, its limits. In the last days of preparation, the brains are few that do not reel under their weight of sudden knowledge; the minds are rare that are not dazzled by their own unaccustomed brilliance. The superlatively trained athlete knocks off for a day or two before an important contest — and perhaps has a dash at the flesh-pots by way of relaxing tension from the snapping point. So does the over-read examinee. He goes home to his sisters and his aunts, and to all the soothing wholesomeness of English country life.

And then that terrible week of incessant examinations! All the facts and any degree of style will fail to save a man unless he has every resource ready at command. No athletic contest, perhaps no battle, could be a severer test of courage. Life does not depend upon the examination, but a living may. In America, degrees are more and more despised; but in England, it still pays to disarrange the alphabet at the end of one's name, or to let it be known to a prospective employer that one is a first-class honor man. The nature of the young graduate's employment and his salary too have a pretty close correspondence with his class at graduation. If he can add a blue to a first, the world is his oyster. The magnitude of the issue makes the examinee — or breaks him. Brilliant and laborious students too often come off with a bare third, and happy audacity has as often brought the careless a first. It may seem that the ordeal is unnecessarily severe; but even here the reason may be found, if it be only granted that the aim of a university is to turn out capable men. The honor examination requires some knowledge, more address, and most of all pluck — pluck or be plucked, as the Cambridge phrase is; and these things in this order are what count in the life of the British Empire.

VI

OXFORD QUALITIES AND THEIR DEFECTS

UNDER the German-American system, the main end is scholarly training. Our graduates are apt to have the Socratic virtue of knowing how little they know — and perhaps not much besides. Even for the scholar this knowledge is not all. Though the English undergraduate is not taught to read manuscripts and decipher inscriptions — to trace out knowledge in its sources — the examination system gives him the breadth of view and mental grasp which are the only safe foundations of scholarship. If he contributes to science, he usually does so after he has left the university. The qualities which then distinguish him are rare among scholars — sound common sense and catholicity of judgment. Such qualities, for instance, enabled an Oxford classical first to recognize Schliemann's greatness while yet the German universities could only see that he was not an orthodox researcher according to their standards. If a man were bent on obtaining the best possible scholarly training, he probably could not do better than to

193

take an English B. A. and then a German or an
American Ph. D. As for the world of deeds and
of men, the knowledge which is power is that
which is combined with address and pluck; and
the English system seems based on practical sense,
in that it lays chief stress on producing this rare
combination.

To attribute to the honor schools the success
with which Englishmen have solved the problems
of civic government and colonial administration
would be to ignore a multitude of contributory
causes; but the honor schools are highly characteristic of the English system, and are responsible
for no small part of its success. A striking illus-
tration of this may be seen in the part which the
periodical press plays in public affairs. In America, nothing is rarer than a writer who combines
broad information with the power of clear and
convincing expression. The editor of any serious American publication will bear me out in the
observation that, notwithstanding the multitude of
topics of the deepest and most vital interest, it is
difficult to find any one to treat them adequately;
and any reader can satisfy himself on this point
by comparing the best of our periodicals with the
leading English reviews. Now the writing of a
review article requires nothing more nor less than

the writing of a first-class examination paper, even to the element of pluck; for to marshal the full forces of the mind in the pressure of public life or of journalism requires self-command in a very high degree. The same thing is as obvious in the daily papers. The world is filled with English newspaper men who combine with reportorial training the power of treating a subject briefly and tellingly in its broadest relations.

The public advantage of this was not long ago very aptly exemplified. When our late war suddenly brought us face to face with the fact that our national destiny had encountered the destinies of the great nations of the world, the most thoughtful people were those who felt most doubt and uncertainty; the more one considered, the less could one say just what he thought. At that crisis a very clear note was sounded. The London correspondents of our papers — Englishmen, and for the most part honor men — presented the issue to us from British and imperialistic point of view with a vigor and conviction that had immediate effect, as we all remember, and gave the larger part of the nation a new view of the crisis, and a new name for it. It was not until weeks later that our own most thoughtful writers as a body perceived the essential difference between our position and that of Great Britain, and we have scarcely yet discarded the word "imperialism." The knowledge, address, and pluck — or shall we call it audacity? — of the English correspondents enabled them to make a stroke of state policy. This is only one of many citable instances.

To the robustious intelligence of the honor man, it must be admitted, the finer enthusiasm of scientific culture is likely to be a sealed book. The whole system of education is against it. Even if a student is possessed by the zeal for research, few tutors, in their pursuit of firsts, scruple to discourage it. "That is an extremely interesting point, but it will not count for schools." One student in a discussion with his tutor quoted a novel opinion of Schwegler's, and was confuted with the remark, "Yes, but that is the German view." It is this tutor who is reported to have remarked: "What I like about my subject is that when you know it you know it, and there's an end of it." His subject was that tangle of falsehood and misconception called history. It must, of course, be remembered in extenuation that with all his social and tutorial duties, the don is very hard worked. And considering the pressure of the necessary preparation for schools, the temptation to shun the byways is very great.

OXFORD QUALITIES AND DEFECTS

The examining board for each school is elected by the entire faculty of that school from its own members; and though it is scarcely possible for an unscrupulous examiner to frame the questions to suit his own pupils, there is nothing to prevent the tutor from framing his pupils' knowledge to meet the presumptive demands of the examiners. " We shall have to pay particular attention to Scottish history, for Scotus is on the board, and that is his hobby." In the school of literæ humaniores, no one expects either pupil or tutor to go far into textual criticism, philology, or archæology. These branches are considered only as regards their results. In history, a special subject has to be studied with reference to its original sources, but its relative importance is small, and a student is discouraged from spending much time on it. Stubbs's " Select Charters " are the only original documents required, and even with regard to these all conclusions are cut and dried.

To be sure there is a science school, but few men elect it, and it is in distinctly bad odor. In the slang of the university it is known as " stinks," and its laboratories as " stink shops." One must admit that its unpopularity is deserved. As it is impossible that each of the twenty colleges should have complete apparatus, the laboratories are maintained by the university, and not well maintained, for the wealth of Oxford is mainly in the coffers of the colleges. The whole end of laboratory work at Oxford is to prepare the student for a "practical examination" of some three hours. The Linacre professor has made many strenuous efforts, and has delivered much pointed criticism, but he has not yet been able to place the school on a modern or a rational basis. In his nostrils, perhaps, more than those of the university, the school of science is unsavory.

Many subjects of the highest practical importance are entirely ignored. No advanced instruction is offered in modern languages and literatures except English, and the school in English is only six years old and very small. No one of the technical branches that are coming to be so prominent a part of American university life is as yet recognized.

The Oxford honor first knows what he knows and sometimes he knows more. Few things are as distressing as the sciolism of a second-rate English editor of a classic. The mint sauce quite forgets that it is not Lamb. The English minor reviewer exhibits the pride of intellect in its purest form. The don perhaps intensifies these amiable foibles. There is an epigram current in Oxford which the

summer guide will tell you Jowett wrote to celebrate his own attainments : —

> Here I am, my name is Jowett;
> I am the master of Balliol College.
> All there is to know, I know it.
> What I know not is not knowledge.

This is clearly a satire written against Jowett, and
it would be more clearly a legitimate satire if
aimed at the generality of dons.

VII

THE UNIVERSITY AND REFORM

THIS tale of Oxford shortcomings is no news to the English radical. The regeneration of the university has long been advocated. On the one hand, the reformers have tried to make it possible, as it was in the Middle Ages, to live and study at Oxford without being attached to any of the colleges; on the other, they have tried to bring into the educational system such modern subjects and methods of study as are cultivated in Germany, where the new branches have been so admirably grafted on the mediæval trunk. In general it must be said that Oxford is becoming more democratic and even more studious; but the advance has come in spite of the constitution of the university. All studied attempts at reform have proved almost ludicrously futile.

In order to combat the monopoly of the colleges, and to build up a body of more serious students without their walls, a new order of "unattached" students was created. The experiment has no doubt been interesting, but it cannot be said that it has revived the glorious democracy and the intellectual enthusiasm of the mediæval university. Few things could be lonelier, or more profitless intellectually, than the lot of the unattached students. Excluded by the force of circumstances from the life of the colleges, they have no more real life of their own than the socially unaffiliated in American universities. They have been forced to imitate the organization of the colleges. They lunch and dine one another as best they can, hold yearly a set of athletic games, and place a boat in the college bumping races. They have thus come to be precisely like any of the colleges, except that they have none of the felicities, social or intellectual, that come from life within walls.

From time to time the introduction of new honor schools is proposed to keep pace with modern learning. A long-standing agitation in favor of a school in modern languages was compromised by the founding of the school in English; but it is not yet downed, and before the century is over may yet rise to smite conservatism. Coupled with this there is an ever-increasing desire to cultivate research. As yet these agitations have had about as much effect as the kindred agitation that led to the rehabilitation of the unattached student.

The Bodleian Library is a treasure chest of the

rarest of old books and of unexplored documents; but nothing in the Bod counts for schools, and so the shadow of an undergraduate darkens the door only when he is showing off the university to his sisters — and to other fellows'. When I applied for permission to read, the fact that I wore a commoner's gown, as I was required to by statute while reading there, almost excluded me. If I had been after knowledge useful in the schools, no doubt I should have been obliged to consult a choice collection of well-approved books across the way in the camera of the Radcliffe. In America, a serious student is welcome to range in the stack, and to take such books as he needs to his own rooms. Some few researchers come to the Bodleian from the world without to spend halcyon days beneath the brave old timber roof of Duke Humphrey's Library; but any one used to the freedom of books in America would find very little encouragement to do so. The librarian is probably an eminently serviceable man according to the traditions of the Bodleian; but there are times when he appears to be a grudging autocrat intrenched behind antique rules and regulations. In the Middle Ages it was the custom to chain the books to the shelves, as one may still observe in the quaint old library of Merton College. The modern method at the Bodleian would seem to be a refinement on the custom. And what is not known about the Bodleian in the Bodleian would fill a library almost as large. In the picture gallery hangs a Van Dyck portrait of William Herbert, Earl of Pembroke, a former chancellor of the university, a nephew of Sir Philip Sydney, son of Mary, Countess of Pembroke, and the once reputed patron to whom Shakespeare addressed the first series of his sonnets. The librarian did not know how or when the portrait came into the possession of the University, or whether it was an original; and not being required to know by statute, he did not care to find out, and did not find out.

The crowning absurdity of the educational system is the professors, and here is an Oxford paradox as yet unredeemed by a glimmering of reason. When I wanted assistance as to a thesis on which I was working, my tutor referred me to the Regius Professor of Modern History, who he thought would be more likely than any one else to know about the sources of Elizabethan literature.

Few as are the professors, they are all too many for the needs of Oxford. They are learned and ardent scholars, many of them with a full measure of German training in addition to Oxford culture. But in proportion as they are wise and able they are lifted out of the life of the university. They lecture, to be sure, in the schools ; and now and then an undergraduate evades his tutor long enough to hear them. Several young women may be found at their feet — students from Somerville and Lady Margaret. When the subject and the lecturer are popular, residents of the town drop in. But as regards the great mass of undergraduates, wisdom crieth in the streets. The professors are as effectually shelved as ever their learned books will be when the twentieth century is dust. "The university, it is true," Mr. Brodrick admits in his "History of Oxford," "has yet to harmonize many conflicting elements which mar the symmetry of its institutions."

This torpor in which the university lies is no mere matter of accident. I quote from Mr. Gladstone's Romanes Lecture, delivered in 1892 : —

"The chief dangers before the English universities are probably two : one that in [cultivating ?] research, considered as apart from their teaching office, they should relax and consequently dwindle [as teachers ?] ; the other that, under pressure from without, they should lean, if ever so little, to that theory of education, which would have it to construct machines of so many horse power rather than to form character, and to rear into true excellence the marvelous creature we call man ; which gloats upon success in life, instead of studying to secure that the man shall ever be greater than his work, and never bounded by it, but that his eye shall boldly run —

Along the line of limitless desire."

Few will question the necessity of rising above the sphere of mere science and commercialism ; but many will question whether the way to rise is not rather by mastering the genius of the century than by ignoring it. It is scarcely too much to say that the greatest intellectual movement of the nineteenth century, though largely the work of English scientists, has left no mark on Oxford education. If, as Professor Von Holst asserts, the American universities are hybrids, Oxford and Cambridge cannot be called universities at all.

VIII

THE UNIVERSITY AND THE PEOPLE

AS a result of the narrowness of the scope of Oxford teaching, the university has no relation to the industrial life of the people — a grave shortcoming in a nation which is not unwilling to be known as a nation of shopkeepers. The wail of the British tradesman is not unfamiliar. Wares " made in Germany " undersell English wares that used to command the market; and being often made of a cheaper grade to suit the demands of purchasers, the phrase " made in Germany " is clearly indicative of fraudulent intention.

Certain instances are exceptionally galling. Aniline dyes were first manufactured from the residuum of coal tar in Great Britain. But enterprising Germany, which has coal-fields of its own, sent apprentices to England who learned the manufacture, and then by means of the chemistry taught in the German universities, revolutionized the process, and discovered how to extract new colors from the coal tar, so that now the bulk of aniline dyes are made in Germany. Obviously, the German chemist is a perfidious person. The Yankee is shrewd and well taught in the technical professions. He makes new and quite unexampled tools, and machinery of all sorts. It takes the Briton some years to be sure that these are not iniquitous — a Yankee trick; but in the end he adopts them. Even then, to the Briton's surprise, the Yankee competes successfully. A commission (no German spy) is sent to America to find out why, and on its return gleefully reports that the Yankee works his tools at a ruinous rate, driving them so hard that in a decade it will be necessary to reëquip his plant entire. At the end of the decade, the conservative Englishman's tools are as good as if they had been kept in cotton batting; but by this time the Yankee has invented newer and more economical devices, and when he reëquips his plant with them he is able to undersell the English producer even more signally. The honest British manufacturer sells his old tools to an unsuspecting brother in trade and adopts the new ones. The Yankee machinist is obviously as perfidious as the German chemist. The upper middle classes in England realize that the destinies of Great Britain and America run together, and they are very hospitable to Americans, but the industrial population hate us scarcely less than they hate the Germans.

All this is, of course, not directly chargeable to the English universities : but the fact remains that in Germany and in America the educational system is the most powerful ally of industry. Here again the English radical is on his guard. From time to time, in letters to the daily papers or political speeches before industrial audiences, the case is very clearly stated. In a recent epistolary agitation in "The Times" it was shown that whereas American and German business men learn foreign languages, Englishmen attempt to sell their wares by means of interpreters, and do not even have their pamphlets and prospectuses translated. Admitting the facts, one gentleman gravely urged that if only the English would stick out the fight, their language would soon be the business language of the world. If it is the conscious purpose of the nation to make it so, it might be of advantage to spell the language as it has been pronounced in the centuries since Chaucer ; already with some such purpose the Germans are adopting Roman characters. But at least it will be many decades before English is the Volapük of business, and meantime England is losing ground. From the point of view of the mere outsider, it would seem of little moment to England what language is used, if the profits of the business transacted accrue to Russian, German, and American corporations.

It has even been strongly urged that commercial and technical subjects be taught in the universities. Cambridge and the University of Glasgow have already a fund with this in view; and the new Midland University at Birmingham, of which Mr. Joseph Chamberlain is chancellor, is to be mainly devoted to commercial science and engineering. It cannot be foretold that the ancient universities will hold their own against the modern. In a speech at Birmingham (January 17, 1901), Mr. Chamberlain said: "Finance is the crux of the situation. Upon our finance depends entirely the extent to which we shall be able to develop this new experiment. With us, in fact, money is the root of all good. I am very glad to say that the promises of donations which, when I last addressed you, amounted to £330,000, have risen since then to an estimated amount of about £410,000. . . . Now £410,000 is a large sum. I heard the other day that the University of Cambridge, which has for some time past been appealing for further assistance, has only up to the present time received £60,000. I most deeply regret that their fund is not larger, and I regret also that ours is so small."

Oxford has apparently not entered the new competition even in a half-hearted manner. For centuries it has been the resort of the nobility and aristocracy, the "governing classes," and though the spirit of the age has so far invaded it as to have been in Mr. Gladstone's eyes its chief danger, the university has as yet only the slenderest connection with the industrial life of the nation.

The virtues of the Oxford educational system, like those of the social and athletic life, are pretty clearly traceable in the main to the division of the university into colleges; at least, it is hard to see how anything other than this could have suggested the idea of having one body to teach the student and another to examine him. And they have a strong family likeness one to another, the concrete result being a highly sturdy and effective character. But the educational system differs from the social and athletic system in that the defects of its qualities are the more vigorous. As far as these defects result from the educational system, they are chargeable not so much to the preponderance of the colleges as to the torpor of the university; and they are powerfully abetted by the Oxford tradition as to the nature and function of a liberal education. This has not always been the case at Oxford. To understand the situation more clearly, it is necessary to review in brief the origin and the growth of the colleges, and the extinction of the mediæval university. This will throw further light on Oxford's social history. We shall thus be better able to judge how **and** to what extent the college system offers a solution for the correction of our American instruction.

IV

THE HISTORY OF THE UNIVERSITY AND THE COLLEGE

I

THE UNIVERSITY BEFORE THE COLLEGE

IN the beginning was the university. The colleges were as unimportant as the university is now. If it be admitted that the university exists to-day, they were less important; for there were no colleges. The origin of the university was probably due to a migration of students in 1167 from the then world-famous University of Paris. The first definite mention of a *studium generale* at Oxford, or assembly of masters of the different faculties, dates from 1185, when Giraldus Cambrensis, as he himself relates, read his new work, "Topographia Hibernia," before the citizens and scholars of the town, and entertained in his hostel "all the doctors of the different faculties."

At this time, and for many centuries afterward, Oxford, like other mediæval universities, was a guild, and was not unlike the trade guilds of the time. Its object was to train and give titles to those who dealt in the arts and professions. The master tanner was trained by his guild to make leather, and he made it; the master of arts was trained by the university to teach, and he taught. He was required to rent rooms in the university schools, for a year and even two, and to show that he deserved his title of master by lecturing in them, and conducting "disputations." The masters lived directly from the contributions of their hearers, their means varying with the popularity of their lectures; and the students were mainly poor clerks, who sought degrees for their money value.

The lectures were mere dictations from manuscript, necessitated by the lack of accessible texts. The students copied the lectures verbatim for future study. The instruction in arts covered the entire field of secular knowledge, the " seven arts," the trivium (grammar, rhetoric, and logic or dialectic), and the quadrivium (music, arithmetic, geometry, and astronomy). The lectures were the main and often the only means of imparting knowledge. The disputations were scholastic arguments — debates — on some set question, and were conducted by the masters. They were the practical application of what the student had learned from the lectures, and were the chief means of intellectual training. Besides attending lectures and disputing, the candidate for the degree had to pass an examination; but the great test of his acquirement seems to have been the skill with which he used his knowledge in debate. Thus the formal disputations occupied very much the same place as the modern written examinations, and they must have required very much the same rare combination of knowledge, address, and pluck. All learning was in a pint-pot; but it was a very serviceable pint-pot.

The university education did not make a man above the work of the world: it made him an engine of so many horse power to perform it. It brought him benefices in that great sphere of activity, the mediæval Church, and important posts in that other sphere of mediæval statecraft, which was so often identified with the Church. If the clerk was above the carpenter, it was not because he came from a different station in life, for he often did not: it was because his work was more important. And he was far above the carpenter. It was a strenuous, glorious life, and the man of intelligence and training found his level, which is the highest. The kings and the nobility were warriors, and may have affected to despise education; but they were far from despising educated men. The machinery of state was organized and controlled by clerks from the university. If the scientific and mechanical professions had existed then, there is no doubt that they would not have been despised as to-day, but would have had full recognition.

Socially, the university was chaos. In the absence of colleges, all the students lived with the townsmen in "chamberdekyns," which appear to be etymologically and historically the forbears of the " diggings " to which the fourth year man now retreats when he has been routed from college by incoming freshmen and by the necessity of reading for his final examination. But such discipline as is now exerted over out-of-college students was undreamed of. In his interesting and profoundly scholarly history of the universities of the Middle Ages, the Rev. Hastings Rashdall gives a vivid picture of mediæval student life, which was pretty much the same in all the universities of Europe. Boys went up to the university at as early an age as thirteen, and the average freshman could not have been older than fifteen; yet they were allowed almost absolute liberty. Drunkenness was rarely treated as a university offense ; and for introducing suspicious women into his rooms, it was only on being repeatedly caught that an undergraduate was disciplined. At the University of Ingolstadt, a student who had killed another in a drunken quarrel had his scholastic effects and garments confiscated by the university. He may have been warned to be good in future, but he was not expelled. "It is satisfactory to add," Rashdall continues, "that at Prague, a Master of Arts, believed to have assisted in cutting the throat of a Friar Bishop, was actually expelled." The body of undergraduates was "an undisciplined student-horde." Hende Nicholas, in Chaucer's "Miller's Tale," is, it must be admitted, a lively and adventuring youth; but he might have been much livelier without being untrue to student life in chamberdekyns.

The townspeople seem to have been the not unnatural fathers of the tradesmen and landlords of modern Oxford; and the likeness is well borne out in the matter of charges. But where to-day a man sometimes tries amiably to beat down the landlord's prices, the way of the Middle Ages was to beat down the landlord. As the student was in many cases of the same station in life as the townsman, he naturally failed to command the servility with which the modern undergraduate is regarded. Both sides used to gird on their armor, and meet in battles that began in bloodshed and often ended in death. Pages of Rashdall's history are filled with accounts of savage encounters between town and gown, which are of importance historically as showing the steps by which the university achieved the anomalous legal dominance over the city which it still in some measure retains. For our present purpose, it is enough to note that mediæval Oxford was unruly, very. "Fighting," says Rashdall, "was perpetually going on in the streets of Oxford. . . . There is probably not a single yard of ground in any part of the classic High Street that lies between St. Martin's and St. Mary's [almost a quarter of a mile] which has not at one time or other been stained with human blood. There are historic battlefields on which less has been spilt."

As if this were not enough, there were civil feuds. In the Middle Ages, sectional differences were more obvious and more important than now; and the first subdivision of the universities, both in England and on the Continent, was by "nations." At Oxford there were two nations; and if, when the north countryman rubbed elbows with the south countryman, he was offended by his silken gown and soft vowels, he rapped him across the pate. Hence more strife and bloodshed. Amid all this disorder there was a full measure of mediæval want and misery. At best, the student of moderate means led a precarious life; and poor students, shivering, homeless, and starved, lived by the still reputable art of the beggar. Something had to be done.

II

THE MEDIÆVAL HALL

THE mediæval spirit of organization, which resulted in so many noble and deathless institutions, was not slow in exerting itself against the social chaos of the university. Out of chaos grew the halls, and out of the halls the colleges. The first permanent organizations of student life were small, and had their origin in the immediate wants of the individual. To gain the economy of coöperation and the safety of numbers, the students at Oxford, as at Paris and elsewhere, began to live in separate small colonies under one roof. These were called aulæ or halls. They were no less interesting in themselves than for the fact that they were the germ out of which the Oxford college system grew.

At first the halls appear to have been mere chance associations. Each had a principal who managed its affairs; but the principal had no official status, and might even be an undergraduate. The halls correspond roughly to the fraternities of American college life. Their internal rule was absolutely democratic. The students lived together by mutual consent under laws of their own framing, and under a principal of their own electing. They were quite without fear or favor of the university. The principal's duties were to lease the hall, to be a sort of over-steward of it, and to lead in enforcing the self-imposed rules of the community. His term of office, like his election, depended on the good-will of his fellows; if he made himself disliked, they were quite at liberty to take up residence elsewhere. In the thirteenth century there was really no such thing as university discipline. The men who lived in the halls came and went as they pleased, and were as free as their contemporary in chamberdekyns to loiter, quarrel, and carouse. Chaucer's "Reeve's Tale" gives us a glimpse into "Soler Halle at Cantebregge," from which it would appear that the members were quite as loose and free as Hende Nicholas, their Oxford contemporary. But the liberty was an organized liberty. In contrast with the chaos of the life of the students in chamberdekyns, the early halls must have been brave places to work and to play in, and one might wish that a fuller record had been left of the life in them. It was their fate to be obscured by the greater splendor and permanence of the colleges to which they paved the way.

III

THE COLLEGE SYSTEM

THE English college, roughly speaking, is a mediæval hall supported by a permanent fund which the socii or fellows administer. The first fund for the support of scholars was bequeathed in 1243, but it can scarcely be regarded as marking the first college, for it provided for two scholars only, and these lived where they pleased. In 1249 William of Durham bequeathed a fund for the support of ten or more masters of arts. At first these also lived apart; it was only in 1280, after the type of the English college had been fixed, that they were formed into the body now known as University College. The first organized community at Oxford was founded by Sir John de Balliol some little time before 1266; but the allowances to the scholars, as was the case in colleges of the University of Paris, after which it was doubtless modeled, were not from a permanent fund, being paid annually by the founder. Balliol cannot therefore be regarded as the first characteristie English college. It was not until 1282 that

Sir John's widow, Dervorguilla, adopted the new English idea by making the endowment of the "House of Balliol" permanent, and placing it under the management of the fellows.

The real founder of the English college was Walter de Merton. In 1264 Walter provided by endowment for the permanent maintenance of twenty scholars, who were to live together in a hall as a community; and in 1274 he drew up the statutes which fix the type of the earliest English college. The principal of Merton was not, like the principal of a mediæval hall, the temporary head of a chance community, but a permanent head with established power; and he had to manage, not the periodic contributions of free associates, but a landed estate held in permanent trust. He was called "warden," a title which the head of Merton retains to this day. This idea of a body supported in a permanent residence by a permanent fund is perhaps of monastic origin, and was accompanied by certain features of brotherhood rule. The scholars lived a life of order and seclusion which was in striking contrast to the life of the students in chamberdekyns, and even of those in the halls. But with the monastic order they had also the monastic democracy, so that in one way the government of the college was strikingly similar to that

NEW COLLEGE CLOISTERS, BELL TOWER, AND CHAPEL

of the halls. Vacancies in the community were filled by coöptation, and the warden was elected by the thirteen senior fellows from their own number. Though partly monastic in constitution, the Hall of Merton was not properly a religious body. The fellows took no vows, and seem rather to have been expected to enter lay callings. This College of Merton was the result of a gradual development of the hall along monastic lines — a lay brotherhood of students. It was destined to work a revolution in English university life and in English university teaching. The constitutions of University and Balliol were, as I have indicated, remodeled on the lines of Merton; and other colleges were founded as follows: Exeter, 1314; Oriel, 1324; Queens, 1341; and Canterbury, now extinct, 1362, most of which were profoundly influenced by the constitution of Merton.

It was at first no part of the duty of the elders (socii, or, as Chaucer calls them, felawes) to teach the younger. The scholars of the college received the regular mediæval education in the university. But even in Merton the germ of tutorial instruction was present. Twelve "parvuli" who were not old enough, or sufficiently used to the Latin tongue, to profit by the lectures and disputations of the university, lived in or near the colleges and were taught by a grammar master; and it appears that even the older scholars might, "without blushing," consult this grammar master on matters that "pertained to his faculty." In his relation to these older students the grammar master may be regarded as the precursor of the system of tutorial instruction.

The first college to develop regular undergraduate instruction within its walls was "S. Marie College of Winchester in Oxford," founded in 1379, by William of Wykeham. "S. Marie's" brought in so many innovations that it came to be called "New College," a title which, incongruously enough, it has retained for more than five hundred years. Wykeham's first innovation was to place the grammar master, for the greater good of his pupils, at the head of a "college" of seventy boys at Winchester, thus outlining the English system of public schools. New College was accordingly able to exclude all who had not attained the ripe age of fifteen. The effect of this innovation on the college was peculiar. When the boys came up from Winchester, they appear to have been farther advanced than most of the undergraduates attending lectures and disputes in the university schools; in any case, Wykeham arranged that the older fellows should supplement the university teaching by private tuition within the college. Little by little the New College type succeeded that of Merton. Magdalen College, founded in 1448, carried the tutorial system to its logical end by endowing lectureships in theology, metaphysics, and natural philosophy. The older colleges — those of the Merton type — little by little followed this new example, so that by the end of the Middle Ages it was possible for a student to receive his entire instruction within the walls of his college. In Wolsey's splendid foundation, Cardinal College (1522), now styled Christ Church, there was a still more ample endowment for professorships. At first the college instruction was regarded as supplementary to the university teaching, though it soon became far more important. The masters of the university continued to read lectures on the recognized subjects, living as of old on fees from those who chose to listen; but they were clearly unable to compete with the endowed tutors and professors of the colleges. By the beginning of the fifteenth century, the mediæval teaching master was disappearing. The only real teaching in arts — by all odds the most popular branch of study at Oxford — was given within the colleges and halls.

The discipline of the earlier colleges was much severer than that of to-day, but the difference is one of degree rather than of kind. The lectures in schools began at six, instead of nine; and at any hour it was forbidden to leave the college except on a studious errand. When attending out-of-college lectures, all scholars were required to go and come in a body; and in one set of statutes even a chaplain was forbidden to leave the gates, except to go to lectures or to the library, without taking at least one companion, who, in the antique phrase of the statute, was to be a "witness of his honest conversation." There were only two meals a day, dinner at ten and supper at five. Breakfast, now the great rallying-point of Oxford hospitality, was the invention of a more luxurious age. Of athletics there was none, or next to none. The only licensed hilarities were certain so-called "honest jokes," with which the tutors were in at least one case required to regale their pupils after dinner, and a "potation" which was permitted after supper, perhaps as an offset to the "honest jokes."

The severity of these regulations is mainly explainable in the fact that the inmates of the colleges were fed, clothed, and housed out of the endowment, and might thus be reasonably expected to give a good account of themselves. Furthermore, they were most of them mere boys. A statute dating as late as 1527 requires that "scholars"

NEW COLLEGE GARDENS

Showing the mediæval wall of Oxford

shall be at least twelve years old. At fourteen or fifteen a scholar might become a fellow. The average age of "determining" as bachelor of arts was little if at all over seventeen. At nineteen, the age at which the modern Oxonian comes up from the public schools, the mediæval student might, if he were clever, be a master of arts, lecturing and disputing in schools for the benefit of the bachelors and scholars of the university.

The modern Oxonian delights to tell visiting friends that he is forbidden by statute to play marbles on the steps of the Bodleian, and to roll hoop in the High; but if a mediæval master of arts were to "come up" to-day, he would be amused, not that so many rules framed for his boyish pupils of old should be applied to grown men, but that the men so obviously require a check to juvenile exuberance. Yet this much has been gained, that the outgrown restrictions of college life have kept Oxford wholesomely young. The survivals of the monastic system meanwhile have kept it wholesomely democratic.

After the colleges reached their full development, the extinction of the mediæval university as an institution for teaching was largely a matter of form. The quietus was given in 1569. The Earl of Leicester, then chancellor, ordered that the

government should be in the hands of the chancellor, doctors, proctors, and the heads of the colleges and halls. In 1636 (the year of the founding of the first American college) the statutes of
the university were revised and codified by Arch-
bishop Laud ; the sole authority was placed in the
hands of an oligarchy composed of the leading
dons of the colleges. The government was limited to the vice-chancellor, the proctors, and the
heads of houses, and the vice-chancellor and the
proctors were elected in sequence by each of the
colleges from its own members. The teaching of
the university was now legally as well as actually
in the hands of the college tutors, and the examination was in the hands of a board chosen by the
colleges. University lectures were still delivered
in the schools by the regent masters, but they had
ceased to play any important part in Oxford education.

IV

THE GOLDEN AGE OF THE MEDIÆVAL HALL

LIKE the colleges, the halls meanwhile tended gradually towards an organized community life. The starting-point was a regulation that the principal should give the university security for the rent of the house. The logical result of this was that the principal became the representative of the university, and the hall one of its recognized institutions. The advantage of living in separate communities meantime had become so clearly evident that by the middle of the fifteenth century chamberdekyns were abolished. All students not living in a college were required to live in a hall. It was thus that the halls lost some of their democratic independence. At this period in their development they may be roughly compared to such modern American halls as Claverly at Harvard, where the residents govern their own affairs in the main, admitting newcomers only by vote, but are all alike subject to the authority of a resident university proctor. The analogy is by no means close, for the principal of the mediæval hall was not so much a resident policeman as the actual head of the community.

As the colleges developed tutorial instruction, the halls followed suit; the local administrator became responsible not only for the social régime, but for the tuition of the undergraduates. The halls thus differed from the college mainly in that they had no corporate existence such as is necessary to an endowed institution. The mediæval hall was now in its golden age; it was a well-conceived instrument for all the purposes of residence and of education. It is especially to be noted that the régime of the community was still in the main democratic. Though the head was appointed by the university, he had to be accepted by vote of the undergraduates, a provision that was still observed, at least in one instance, until the close of the nineteenth century.

The discipline of the halls of the fifteenth century, severe though it was by comparison with that of the earliest halls, was far less severe than the discipline in the colleges. It was quite as much as the university could accomplish, according to Rashdall, " to prevent students expelled from one hall being welcomed at another, to prevent the masters themselves condoning or sharing the worst excesses of their pupils, to compel fairly regular attendance at lectures and other university or college exercises, to require all students to return home by curfew at 8 or 9 P. M., to get the outer doors of the pedagogy locked till morning, and to insist on the presence of a regent throughout the night." When the early habits of the community generally are remembered, it will be evident that these regulations still allowed a vast deal of liberty, or rather of license. Boys of fifteen or sixteen living in the very centre of large and densely populated towns were in general perfectly free to roam about the streets up to the hour at which all respectable citizens were accustomed, if not actually compelled by town statutes, to retire to bed.

The halls were reduced in number by the wars of the Roses and by a period of intellectual stagnation that followed, but they still numbered seventy-one, as against eighteen colleges (including those maintained by monasteries, which disappeared with the Reformation) ; and the number of their students is estimated at seven hundred, as against three hundred in the colleges. In the light of subsequent development it seems probable that it would have been far better for the university if the halls had remained the characteristic subdivision. Their fate was decided not by any inherent superiority on the part of the colleges, but by the force of corporate wealth.

Even in the fifteenth century, the halls were tending to pass into the possession of the colleges, and later events made the tendency a fact. "As stars lose their light when the sun ariseth," says an ancient Cambridge worthy, "so all these hostels decayed by degrees when endowed colleges began to appear." The Reformation, and a recurrent pestilence, "the sweating sickness," a kind of inflammatory rheumatism due apparently to the unwholesome situation of the university, resulted in a sharp falling off in the number of students. The colleges lived on, however thinned their ranks, by virtue of the endowments; but the halls disappeared with the students who had frequented them. In 1526 it was recorded that sixteen had lately been abandoned. When the numbers of the university swelled again under Elizabeth, the increase found place partly in the few halls that were left, but mainly in the colleges. In 1602 there were only eight halls, and these were all mere dependencies of separate colleges. "*Singulæ singulis a colegiis pendent*," as a contemporary expresses it. Only one of these, St. Edmund Hall, now retains even a show of the old democratic independence, and this has lately been brought into closer subjection to Queen's College. Socially as well as educationally, the mediæval university faded before the organization and endowment of the colleges. The life of Oxford was concentrated in a dozen or more separate institutions, and so thoroughly concentrated that there was little association, intellectual or social, between any two of them.

V

THE ORIGIN OF THE MODERN UNDER-
GRADUATE

IF the tutors of New College were epoch-mak-
ing, the amplitude and splendor of its social
life were no less so. Its original buildings are in
such perfect preservation that it is hard to believe
that they are almost the oldest in Oxford, and
that the New College quadrangle is the father of
all quads. The establishment of the "head" was
of similar dignity. The master of Balliol received
forty shillings yearly; the warden of New College,
forty pounds. In the statutes of an old Cambridge college we find it required that since it
would be "indecent" for the master to go afoot,
and "scandalous" to the college for him to "con-
ducere hackeneye," he might be allowed one horse.
The warden of New College had a coach and six.
As century followed century the value of the endowments increased, and the scale of living was
proportionately raised. The colleges in general
became the home of comfort, and sometimes of a
very positive luxury.

THE MODERN UNDERGRADUATE

In the colleges of the Middle Ages the students were the *socii*, and were maintained by the endowment. These are the dons and foundationers, or scholarship men, of to-day. But the comfort and order of the life in the colleges were very attractive, and the sons of the rich were early welcomed as "gentlemen commoners," precursors of the modern "commoners." The statutes of Magdalen make the first clear provision for receiving and teaching such "non-foundation" students. They permit the admission of twenty *filii nobilium* as *commensales*, or commoners, in the vernacular. At first these were few and unimportant; in the centuries during which the numbers of the university were at an ebb, they could easily be accommodated within the depleted colleges. When the university increased under Elizabeth, the idea of living in halls in the mediæval fashion, as we have seen, was obsolescent, so that the result of the increase was to enlarge the colleges. Thus, largely as a matter of chance, the commoners of to-day, the characteristic and by far the larger part of the undergraduate body, live under a régime invented for the endowed scholars of the Middle Ages, and the democratic license of the mediæval undergraduate at large has given way to a democratic rule of commoners in colleges. Though the commoner is no longer called a gentleman commoner, he is more than likely to come from a family of position and means, for the comfort of life in the colleges is expensive. All this has transformed Oxford from a mediæval guild of masters and apprenticed students, a free mart of available knowledge, into a closely organized anteroom to social and professional life.

VI

THE INSIGNIFICANCE OF THE MODERN UNIVERSITY

THOUGH the university as a teaching body pined before the rising colleges, and for centuries lay in a swoon, it was not dead. It was kept alive by certain endowments for lecturers. But so thoroughly did the college tutors supply all undergraduate needs that, unless walls indeed have ears, the lectures were never heard. The professors gradually abandoned the university schools and gave the unattended lectures in their own houses. Such lectures were known as " study lectures." Even these gave way to silence. An odd situation was caused by the fact that there were also salaries paid to university proctors, a part of whose duty it was to see that the professorial lectures were properly given. When a proctor appeared, the learned professor would snatch up his manuscript and read until his auditor got tired and left. This was one case in which a thief was not the person to catch a thief; such energy on the part of the proctor was unusual, and was regarded as in extremely bad form. The abuse proceeded so far that in some cases, when hearers appeared at the appointed hour, the professors refused point blank to read their lectures. The climax of the farce was that at graduation students were fined for having cut these lectures that had never been given. When Samuel Johnson was fined for neglecting a college lecture to go " sliding on Christ Church Meadow," he exclaimed, " Sir, you have fined me twopence for missing a lecture that was not worth a penny!" His untimely departure from Oxford has lamentably left us to conjecture what he would have said upon paying the university fines at graduation for cutting lectures that had never been given.

Even the university examinations became farcical. Under the Laudian statutes the very examiners became corrupt. Instead of a feast of reason and a flow of soul, the wary student provided his examiner with good meat and wine ; and the two, with what company they bade in, got gloriously drunk together. B. A. meant Bacchanal of Arts. Even when the forms of examination were held to, the farce was only less obvious. A writer in *Terræ Filius*, March 24, 1721, tells us that the examination consisted in " a formal repetition of a set of syllogisms upon some ridiculous question in logick, which the candidates get by rote, or perhaps read out of their caps, which lie before them." These commodious sets of syllogisms were called strings, and descended from undergraduate to undergraduate in a regular succession like themes and mechanical drawings in an American club or fraternity. "I have in my custody a book of strings upon most or all of the questions discussed in a certain college noted for its ratiocinative faculty; on the first leaf of which are these words: *Ex dono Richardi P——e primæ classi benefactoris munificentissimi*." Lord Eldon took his degree at University College by an examination that consisted of two questions: "What is the meaning of Golgotha?" and "Who founded University College?" It was, no doubt, the bearers of degrees thus achieved who owned those marvelous libraries of the eighteenth century, which consisted of pasteboard boxes exquisitely backed in tooled calf, and labeled with the names of the standard Greek and Latin classics.

The decline of the university teaching and examination did not result in a corresponding rise in the colleges. Each of the dozen and more institutions was supposed, as I have said, to keep a separate faculty in arts, and often in law and theology as well. If there had been any incentive to ambition, the colleges might have vied with one another in their impossible task, or at least have gone far enough to bring about a reform. But they were rich and did not care. The wealth of collegiate endowments, that had begun by ruining the university, ended by ruining the colleges. There were still earnest teachers and students at Oxford, but they were not the rule. The chief energies of the tutors were spent in increasing their salaries by a careful management of the estates, and in evading their pupils. In "the splendid foppery of a well-turned period" Gibbon thus pictures the dons of Magdalen in 1752: "Their deep and dull potations excused the brisk intemperance of youth." Only one result was possible. In 1821 T. J. Hogg, Shelley's college-mate at University College, referred to Oxford as a seat of learning. "Why do you call it so?" Shelley cried indignantly. "Because," Hogg replied, "it is a place in which learning sits very comfortably, well thrown back as in an easy chair, and sleeps so soundly that neither you nor I nor anybody else can wake her." Permanent endowments had transferred the seat of learning from a nobly indigent university to the colleges, and the deep and dull potations of endowed tutors had put it asleep on the common-room chairs.

The nineteenth century did not altogether arouse

it. "The studies of the university," according to the testimony of the Oxford Commission of 1850, "were first raised from their abject state by a statute passed in 1800." Heretofore all students had pursued the same studies, and there was no distinction to be gained at graduation except the mere fact of becoming a Bachelor of Arts. The statute of 1800 provided that such students as chose might distinguish themselves from the rest by taking honors; and for both passman and honor man it provided a dignified and quite undebauchable university examining board. At first the subjects studied were, roughly speaking, the same for passman and honor man; the difference was made by raising the standard of the honor examination. The examination followed the mediæval custom in being mainly oral; and though it soon came to be written, it still preserves the tradition of the mediæval disputation by including a *viva voce* which is open to the attendance of the public. Throughout the nineteenth century the development consisted mainly in adding a few minor schools.

The good and bad features of the English college system as a whole should not be hard to distinguish. In all social aspects the colleges are as nearly perfect as human institutions are capable of becoming, and they are the foundation of an unequaled athletic life. Educationally, their qualities are mixed. For the purpose of common or garden English gentlemen, nothing could be better than a happy combination of tutorial instruction and university examining. For the purposes of scholarly instruction in general, and of instruction in the modern sciences and mechanic arts in particular, few things could be worse than the system as at present construed.

To exult over the superiority of American institutions in so many of the things that make up a modern university would not be a very profitable proceeding. Let us neglect the imperfections of Oxford. It is of much greater profit to consider the extraordinary social advantages that arise from the division of the university into colleges, and the educational advantages of the honor schools. These are points with regard to which we are as poor as Oxford is poor in the scope of university instruction.

The point will perhaps be clearer for a brief review of the manner in which our college system grew out of the English. The development is the reverse of what we have just been considering. In England, the colleges overshadowed the university and sapped its life. With us, the university has overshadowed the college and is bidding fair to annihilate it.

VII

THE COLLEGE IN AMERICA

IN 1636 the Commonwealth of Massachusetts passed an act to establish a " schoole or colledge," and set apart a tract of land in " New Towne " as its seat, which they called Cambridge. Our Puritan forefathers had carried from the English university the conviction that " sound learning " is the " root of true religion," and were resolved, in their own vigorous phrase, that it should not be " buried in the graves of the fathers." In 1638 a master of arts of Emmanuel College, Cambridge, John Harvard, bequeathed to the new institution his library and half his fortune, some £780. A timber building was erected and a corporation formed which bore the donor's name. From the regulations in force in 1655 it is evident that in its manner of life, its laws of government, the studies taught, and the manner of granting the degree, Harvard College was a close counterpart of the English college of the early seventeenth century, its very phraseology including such terms as " disputing," " proceeding," " determining." It was the first institution of higher education in British America. Until the founding of the first state university, the University of Virginia, in 1819, the constitution afforded the principal model for subsequent foundations, and to-day colleges of the Harvard type are perhaps the strongest factor in American education. Harvard thus transplanted to American soil the full measure of the traditions of the Middle Ages, many of which exist in a modified form to-day.

In "Harvard College by an Oxonian" Dr. George Birkbeck Hill suggests that John Harvard expected others to found similar institutions which collectively were to reproduce the University of Cambridge in New England. The supposition is by no means impossible, and the manuscript records in the Harvard Library would perhaps reward research. But whatever the intention, it is abundantly clear that in the full English sense of the word no second college was established at Cambridge. The first constitution was in all essentials the same as that of to-day. Hutchinson's "History of Massachusetts" records (1676): "There are but four fellowships, the two seniors have each 30*l.* per ann. and the two juniors 15*l.*, but no diet is allowed: There are tutors to all such as are admitted students. . . . The government of these colledges is in the governor and magistrates of Massachusetts and the president of the colledge, together with the teaching elders of the six adjacent towns." The fellows are the forbears of the modern corporation, the tutors of the faculty; and though the institution has been separated from the state, the "teaching elders" are the earliest overseers. Furthermore, the endowment of Harvard has remained undivided; and generations elapsed before the present very un-English division was made by which the teaching force is separated into independent faculties for arts and the various professions. From the first the "college" was a "university" in that it granted degrees; and less than twenty years after its founding the two terms are used as synonymous; an appendix to what is called the charter of Harvard "College" calls the institution a "University." This confusion of terms still persists, and is found at most other American institutions, the constitutions of which were largely modeled after that of Harvard. For generations the endowments and the teaching force of the American college and university were identical. Thus as regards its constitution the typical American university is a single English college writ large.

Almost from the outset, however, there were, in one sense of the word, several colleges. In "An

Inventory of the whole Estate of Harv^d Colledge taken by the President & Fellows as they find the same to be Decemb. 10, 1654," the first two items are as follows : —

" Imp^rs. The building called the old colledge, conteyning a Hall, Kitchen, Buttery, Cellar, Turrett & 5 Studeys & therin 7 chambers for students in them. A Pantry & small corne Chamber. A library & Books therin, vallued at 400^lb.

"It. Another house called Goffes colledge, & was purchased of Edw: Goffe. conteyning five chambers. 18 studyes. a kitchen cellar & 3 garretts." [1]

It is to be noted that " Old Colledge," which was Harvard's building, had a kitchen, buttery, and cellar, a pantry and a small corn chamber, and was thus primitively modeled after an English hall or college. Presumably the inmates, like their cousins across the water, dined in the hall. As for " Goffe's colledge," granting that the punctuation of the inventory is intentional, it had a kitchen cellar, which would seem to imply a kitchen; and it is not impossible that there should be a comma after " kitchen." No hall is mentioned, and it is hardly likely that there could have been so imposing a room in what was built

[1] William G. Brown in *The Nation*, vol. 61, No. 1585, p. 346.

for a private house; but it would have been possible and natural to serve meals in the largest of the five "chambers." A third building Hutchinson's history describes as "a small brick building called the Indian Colledge, where some few Indians did study, but now it is a printing house," the first printing house in British America. The two earliest buildings at Harvard would thus be the abodes of separate communities, and though I can find no intimation as to the Indian College, it can scarcely be doubted that since it was established for the separate use of the redskins, it contained a separate living-plant. A later record shows that there was a separate kitchen in the first Stoughton Hall.

These early "colledges" at Harvard are more properly termed halls, and such as survived are now so called. They had probably little in common with the democratic English halls of the Middle Ages. Both at Oxford and at Cambridge the halls of the seventeenth century were, as I have said, mere pendants of the colleges; they must have had a separate character as a social community and a certain independence; but if they had separate endowments, they did not manage them, and each of them depended for its instruction mainly on the college to which it was affiliated. The printed records of the early American halls are

249

too meagre to warrant definite conclusions; but they seem to show that the halls were conceived in the spirit of the English hall of the seventeenth century, in that they provided for separate social and residential communities without separate endowment or teaching force. If the increase of students at Harvard had been rapid, it is not unlikely that many new halls would have been established, each the home of a complete community; but for half a century the number fluctuated between fifteen and thirty. If we take the English estimate of two hundred and fifty as the largest feasible size for a single community, the limit was not reached until as late as 1840. By 1676 the timber "colledge" built at the charge of Mr. Harvard, which bore his name, had been superseded by the first Harvard Hall, which Hutchinson describes as "a fair pile of brick building covered with tiles by reason of the late Indian warre not yet finished. . . . It contains twenty chambers for students, two in a chamber, a large hall which serves for a chapel; over that a convenient library." In these ample accommodations it was found that the student body could be most conveniently and cheaply fed as a single community. Thus, like the idea of a group of colleges with separate finances and teaching bodies, the idea of separate residential halls must have passed away with the generation of divines educated in England. The American college and the American university remained identical, not only educationally and in their finances, but as a social organization. This fact has caused a curious reversion in America toward the mediæval type of university, both socially and educationally.

As the university has expanded, it has declined socially: to-day the residential life is only a degree better than that in the ancient chamberdekyns. Educationally, the reversion has been fortunate: the university is alive to the needs of the life about it. If it here resembles the modern German universities, this is largely due to the fact that both have more faithfully preserved the system and the spirit of the Middle Ages: the resemblance is quite as much a matter of native growth in America as of foreign imitation. In England, the mediæval idea of a multiplicity of residential bodies has survived, and the educational idea of the mediæval university has perished. In Germany, the educational idea has survived, and the old community life has perished. In America, the two ideas have survived by virtue of their identity. But for the same reason both are in a rudimentary and very imperfect state of development.

251

V

THE PROBLEMS OF THE AMERICAN UNIVERSITY

THE SOCIAL AND ATHLETIC PROBLEM

THE imperfection of the modern American university in its social organization has been stated with the utmost clearness and authority, at least as regards Harvard. The " Harvard Graduates' Magazine " for September, 1894, published posthumously an article by Frank Bolles, late secretary of the college, entitled " The Administrative Problem." " In the present state of affairs," says Mr. Bolles, " student social life is stunted and distorted. . . . There is something very ugly in the possibility of a young man's coming to Cambridge, and while here sleeping and studying alone in a cheerless lodging, eating alone in a dismal restaurant, feeling himself unknown, and so alone in his lectures, his chapel, and his recreations, and not even having the privilege of seeing his administrative officers, who know most of his record, without having to explain to them at each visit who he is and what he is, before they can be made to remember that he is a living, hoping, or despairing part of Harvard College."

Some of these men who fail to find a place in the social community meet their isolation grimly and are embittered against life. Others, after a few months or a year of lonesomeness and neglect, give up their university career broken-hearted, and by so doing perhaps take the first step in a life of failures. One man of whom I happened to know confided to his daily themes a depth of misery of which it can only be hoped that it was hysterical. At night when he heard a step on his staircase he prayed that it might be some one coming to see him. The tide of undergraduate life and of joy in living flowed all about him and left him thirsting. If a man finds sweetness in the uses of such adversity, it can only be by virtue of the firmest and calmest of tempers. Sometimes fellows starve physically without a friend with whom to share their hardship, living perhaps on bread, milk, and oatmeal, which they cook over the study lamp. Occasionally one hears disquieting rumors that such short rations have resulted in disease and even death before the authorities were aware. If this be so, the hardships of life in the earliest mediæval university, though far enough removed from us to be picturesque, could hardly have been more real.

The sickness of the body politic has been por-

trayed with artistic sympathy and veracity by Mr.
C. M. Flandrau, in his "Harvard Episodes,"
the wittiest and most searching of studies of undergraduate life. It is no doubt for this reason
that the book is both read and resented by the
healthy and unthinking college man.

To dwell on such individual instances would be
unpleasant. The point of importance is to show
how the social chaos affects the health of the
community as a whole. As it happens, we have a
barometer. For better or for worse, the moving
passion of the undergraduate body, aside from
studies, is athletic success. If athletics prosper, it
is because the life of the college finds an easy and
natural expression; if athletics languish, there is
pretty sure to be some check on wholesome functioning.

The causes of Harvard's abundant failures and
the remedies have been a fertile theme of discussion.
One cause is obvious. The rivals with distressing frequency have produced better teams. Every
one knows that what Cambridge chooses to call
Yale luck is nine parts Yale pluck; and the quality is well developed at Princeton, Pennsylvania,
and elsewhere. But why is it developed at these
places more than at Harvard? The explanations
are legion. The first cry was bad coaching. This

was repeated until the fault was corrected, at least in part, and until every one was wholly tired of hearing the explanation. Then came the cry of bad physical training. This in turn was repeated until it brought partial remedy and total weariness of the agitation. By and by, all other complaints having been worn threadbare, Harvard's defeat was attributed to the fog on Soldier's Field. It is not unlikely that the fog will be dissipated and the athletes duly benefited. Yet it is far from certain that this will make the athletic body sound.

The fault lies deeper than Yale pluck — or even the fog on Soldier's Field. It is to be found in the conditions, social, administrative, and even educational, which are at the basis of the life of the university. If these conditions were peculiar to Harvard, it would decidedly not be worth while to discuss them publicly. But they are inherent in the type of university of which Harvard is the earliest and most developed example, and are destined to crop out in every American institution of learning in proportion as it grows, as Harvard has grown, from the English college of a few decades ago into the Teutonized university of the present and of the future. In considering the causes, it is necessary to speak concretely of our one eminent example; but the main fact brought out will be applicable in greater or less degree to the present or future of any American college.

The sources of Harvard's weakness are mainly social. When the college was small, it had its share of victory; but almost from the year when it began to outgrow its rivals, its prowess declined. Forty years ago, and even less, the undergraduate constitution of American institutions was, roughly speaking, that of the colleges of Oxford and Cambridge: a freshman was measurably sure of falling into easy relationship with the fellows of his class and of other classes, and thus of finding his level or his pinnacle in athletic teams and in clubs. Considered as a machine for developing good fellows and good sportsmen, it was well adjusted and well oiled; it worked. But it was not capable of expansion. Two or three hundred fellows can live and even dine together with comfort and an increase of mutual understanding; they soon become an organized community. When a thousand or two live as a single community and dine at one board (let us call it dining), the social bond relaxes. Next door neighbors are unknown to one another, having no common ground of meeting, and even the college commons fail to bring them together. The relaxing influence of the hour spent at table and in the subsequent conversation, during which social intercourse should most freely flourish, is quite lost. The undergraduate body is a mob, or at best an aggregation of shifting cliques. If men live in crowds or in cliques, their life is that of crowds or of cliques, and is unprofitable both to themselves and to the community that should prosper by their loyal activity.

It is true that there are societies and clubs, but these also to a certain degree have been swamped in the rising tide of undergraduates. With freshman classes as large as those of to-day, the old social machinery becomes incapable of sifting the clubable from the less clubable, those who deserve recognition in the body of undergraduates from those who do not. The evil is increased by the fact that as a rule in America the social life is organized early in the undergraduate course, so that the men who fail of election in the first year or two have failed for good. There are, to be sure, cases in which men who have later developed signal merit have been taken into the all-important societies and clubs of the upper classmen, and sometimes these societies make a special and most creditable effort thus to remedy the failures of the system; but the men who are thus elected are an exception, and an exception of the kind that proves the rule. Unless a man has been prominent in one of the large preparatory schools, or becomes prominent in athletics in the first year or so, there is only one way to make sure of meeting such fellows as he wishes to know, and that is both to choose friends and to avoid them with an eye to social chances, a method which is scarcely to be commended. As the incoming classes grow larger, there is an increasingly large proportion of undergraduates who fail to qualify in the first year or two in any of these ways. Throughout their course they neither receive benefit from the general life of the university nor contribute to it. They are often of loyal and disinterested character, and they not infrequently develop into men of exceptional ability in all of the paths of undergraduate life; not a few of them have been 'varsity captains. But instead of exerting the influence on the welfare of the university which such men might and should exert, they find it impossible to get into the main currents, and revolve impotently on the outside, each in the particular eddy where fate has thrust him.

At Harvard, where the evil has long been recognized, a remedy has been sought in increasing the membership of the great sophomore and senior societies, the Institute of 1770 and the Hasty Pudding Club. The result has been the reverse of what was intended. The larger the club the less compact its life and its influence, — what a few men have gained the club has lost. The tendency toward disintegration is confirmed by a peculiarity of the organization of the societies. The first half of the members of the Institute form a separate club, the D. K. E., or Dickey. From this the second half are excluded, becoming a sort of social fringe; they often form a part of the mob that dines at Memorial or of the cliques that dine in boarding-houses, and are only a shade less excluded than the rest from the centres of the college life. If this inner club, the Dickey, were the instrument of a united and efficient public spirit, the case would not be so bad, but its members in turn are split into a number of small clubs; as a social organization the Dickey is mainly a name. If now these small clubs took a strong part in the general life of the college, the case would still not be so bad; but each spends its main strength in struggling with the others to secure as many members as possible from the first ten of the Dickey. They are scarcely to be regarded as engines of public spirit.

The same is true of the great senior society, the Hasty Pudding. Its most prominent members belong to the few small clubs of upper classmen; the rest are as much a social fringe as the later tens of the Institute. And the senior clubs, like the clubs of the under classmen, are more interested in their private politics than in the policy of the college as a whole. At Yale the senior societies still exert a strong and generally wholesome influence, but at Harvard they have long ceased to do so, if they ever did. In proportion as a man is successful in the social world the system lifts him out of the body of undergraduate life. The reward of athletic distinction or of good-fellowship is a sort of pool pocket, upon getting into which a man is definitely out of the game. The leaders in the college life, social and athletic, are chosen on the superficial tests of the freshman year, and are not truly representative; and the organization of which they become a part is calculated only to suppress general and efficient public spirit. The outer layers are dead wood and the kernels sterile. This is at least one reason why Harvard does not oftener win.

In all this there is no place for a philosophy of despair. The spirit of the undergraduate, clubbed and unclubbed, is normal and sound. The efforts which the clubs themselves make from time to time to become representative are admirably public spirited; and there is no less desire on the part of the outsiders to live for the best interests of the college. On the day of an athletic contest the university is behind the team, heart and lungs; and when defeat comes it is felt alike by all conditions of men. From time to time ancient athletes journey to Cambridge to exhort the undergraduate body to pull together; and it is a poor orator indeed who cannot set in motion strong currents of enthusiasm. Half an hour of earnest talk on the strenuous life from Theodore Roosevelt has often been known to raise a passion of aspiration that has positively lasted for weeks. But the social system cannot be galvanized into life and functioning. The undergraduates aspire and strive, but every effort is throttled by a Little Old Man of the Sea. When all is said and done, the mob and the cliques remain mob and cliques; with discord within and exclusive without, there is small hope of organized efficiency.

At Yale the oligarchic spirit of the senior societies is compact and operative where that of the Harvard clubs is not; but Yale also is being swamped. The vast and increasing mob of the unaffiliated has several times within the last decade shown a shocking disrespect for the sacred authority of the captains; and the non-representative character of the sophomore societies, from which the senior societies are recruited, has been a public scandal. One result of this disorder is that the ancient athletic prestige is slipping away, or is so far in abeyance that it is again a question whether Harvard or Yale has — shall we say the worse team? The case of the older universities is typical. Other institutions are expanding as fast or faster, and it is only a question of time when the increase of numbers will swamp the social system.

That there is something rotten in the state of Denmark has of late been officially recognized, at least at Harvard. In order to create a general social and athletic life in the community a Union has been established, modeled on the Oxford Union. It would be pleasant to picture the College House of the future shaking hands with Claverly, the Phi Beta Kappa linking elbows with the Porcellian, and the fellows who now, in spite of a desire to be sociable, have lived through four years of solitary confinement each in his petty circle, enjoying the bosom friendship of all the men they may desire to know. It would be pleasant but perhaps not altogether warrantable, when one considers the essential nature of the Union.

The Oxford Union of celebrity, as has been

pointed out in an earlier chapter, is a thing of the past. It was an exclusive institution, in which no attempt was made to foster universal brotherhood. When it was thrown open to the entire undergraduate world, it lost caste and authority. The elect flocked by themselves each in his own exclusive club. If the Harvard Union had been modeled on the old exclusive Oxford Union, it might perhaps have been equally efficient in bringing together a broadly representative body of men. But it was modeled on the modern democratic Union. Here is a plain case: When the Oxford Union ceased to be exclusive, its best elements flocked by themselves, and the result is a growth of small exclusive clubs. At Harvard the exclusive clubs and societies are both ancient and honorable, and, moreover, very comfortable, and it hardly seems likely that their members will rout themselves out of their cosy corners to join the merry rout at the Harvard Union.

This is not to cast a gloomy eye upon the new university club; it is rather by way of emphasizing the importance of the work it has to do, and will succeed in doing. Hitherto the lounging grounds of the unaffiliated (alas! that in such an alma mater so many are forever unaffiliated!) have been public billiard-rooms and tobacco shops.

For the solace of a midnight supper one had to go to the locally familiar straw-hatted genius of the sandwich, and for the luxury of a late breakfast to John of the Holly Tree. And John the Orange Man! Great worthies these, ancient and most honorable. But even in the enchantment of retrospect they somehow or other explain why so many fellows choose to live, for the most part, in small cliques in one another's rooms and cultivate the deadly chafing-dish. For the unaffiliated — by far the larger part of each class — the new club-house will be a Godsend. It is much more fun to cut a nine-o'clock lecture if you are sure of a comfortable chair at breakfast and a real napkin; and even in the brutal gladness of youth, it is pleasant at a midnight supper to be seated. And then, after that athletic dinner at Memorial, a place to loaf quietly over a pipe with whatever congenial spirit one finds, and listen to the clicking of billiard-balls! It is also proposed that the 'varsity athletes have their training tables at the new Union, so that any fellow may come to know them clothed and in their right minds. I fancy that the new club will leave those old worthies a trifle lonesome, and will banish the chafing-dish forever.

The spirit of an old graduate somehow takes kindly to the idea of a place like that. How the spirit of Bishop Brooks, for instance, would enjoy slipping in of an evening for the cigar they have denied him in the house erected in his memory! And for the graduate in the flesh the club-house will be no less welcome, especially if he is unlucky enough not to have a club of his own to go back to. To love one's alma mater it is, of course, not necessary to have a club; but it somehow interferes with the sentiment of a home-coming to be obliged to go back to Boston by trolley for luncheon and dinner, and to eat it among aliens. In the new Union it will even be possible to put up for the night. A long step has been made in advance of the old unhappy order. Yet the new Union leaves the vital evil in the community life as far as ever from solution.

What the authorities have failed to do consciously may, according to present indications, be accomplished, in some manner at least, by an unconscious growth. When Memorial became inadequate to the mere demand for seating-room, new dining-halls were established. In the future it is possible that these new halls may be kept within the line where community life becomes impossible and mob life begins. If they could be, the problem would be at least one step nearer solution. But to gain the highest effect of community organi-

268

zation, it is necessary that the men who dine in the same hall shall live near one another. Under the present system this rarely happens, and when it does, it does not even follow that they know one another by sight. Until the halls represent some real division in undergraduate life — separate and organized communities — they must remain the resort of a student mob.

Fortunately, another movement is discernible in the direction of separate residential organization. Already certain of the dormitories in American universities are governed democratically by the inmates : no student is admitted except by order of a committee of the members. The fraternity houses so widely diffused in America offer a still better example, almost a counterpart, of the halls of the golden age of the mediæval university. Any considerable development of hall or fraternity life in the great universities would result in a dual organization of the kind that has proved of such advantage in England, so that a man would have his residence in a small democratic community, and satisfy his more special interests in the exclusive clubs of the university. In such an arrangement the hall would profit by the clubman as the clubman would gain influence through the hall. All undergraduates would thus be united in the gen-

eral university life in a way which is now undreamed of, and which is unlikely, as I think, even
in the new Harvard Union.

The tendency toward division in the dining-halls
and the dormitories is evident also in athletics;
but here it is very far from unconscious. The
division by classes long ago ceased to be an adequate means of developing material for the 'varsity
teams, and when the English rowing coach, Mr. R.
C. Lehmann, was in charge of the Harvard oarsmen, he outlined a plan for developing separate
crews not unlike the college crews of England.
This system has since been effected with excellent
results. Separate boating clubs have been established, each of which has races among its own
crews and races with the crews of its rivals. Only
one thing has prevented the complete success of
the system. The division into clubs is factitious,
representing no real rivalry such as exists among
English colleges. To supply this rivalry, it is
only necessary that each boat club shall represent
a hall. The same division would of course be
equally of benefit in all branches of sport. The
various teams within the university would then
represent a real social rivalry, such as has long
ceased to exist. This could scarcely fail to produce the effect that has been so remarkable at the

English universities. As in England, a multiplication of contests would on the one hand develop far better university material, and on the other hand it would lessen rather than exaggerate the excessive importance of intercollegiate contests.

II

THE ADMINISTRATIVE PROBLEM

THE administrative evil of the American university, as typified in Harvard, Mr. Bolles described even more vividly than the social evil. The bare fact of the problem he stated as follows: " In 1840 the college contained 250 students; in 1850, 300; in 1860, 450; in 1870, 600; in 1880, 800; in 1890, 1300; in 1894, 1600." He then pointed out that the only means the authorities have found for meeting this increasing demand on the administrative office is, not to divide the students into separate small bodies each under a single administrator, but to divide the duties of administration among several officers. Thus each of the added officers is required to perform his duty toward the entire student body. It is apparently assumed that he can discharge one duty toward two or three thousand students as intelligently as in former years he could discharge two or three duties toward two or three hundred. By this arrangement the most valuable factor in administration is eliminated — personal knowledge and personal contact between

272

the administrator and his charges. It is said that the members of the administrative board of the college — professors whose time is of extreme value to the university and to the world, and who receive no pay as administrators — sit three hours a night three nights in the week deciding the cases that come before them, not from personal knowledge of the undergraduates concerned, but from oral and documentary reports. " It is only by a fiction that the Recorder [or the Dean, or the member of the administrative board] can be assumed to have any personal knowledge of even a half of the men whose absences. he counts, whose petitions he acts upon, and against whose delinquencies he remonstrates ; yet the fiction is maintained while its absurdity keeps on growing. . . . If the rate of growth and our present administrative system are maintained, the Dean and Recorder of Harvard College will [in 1950] be personally caring for 6500 individuals, with all of whom they will be presumed to have an intelligent acquaintance."

Mr. Bolles lived through the period in which a brilliant band of German-trained American professors, having made over our educational system as far as possible on German lines, were endeavoring to substitute German discipline, or lack of it, for the traditional system of collegiate residence which aims to make the college a well-regulated social community. At one time these reformers rejoiced in the fact that Harvard students attended the ice carnival at Montreal or basked in the Bermudan sun while the faculty had no means of knowing where they were and no responsibility for the success of their college work. The Overseers, however, were not in sympathy with the Teutonized faculty, and soon put an end to this; but the reformers were, and perhaps still are, only waiting the opportunity to establish again the Teutonic license. " It is sometimes said," Mr. Bolles continues, " that Harvard may eventually free itself from all its remaining parental responsibility and leave students' habits, health, and morals to their individual care, confining itself to teaching, research, and the granting of degrees. Before it can do this, it must be freed from dormitories. As long as fifteen hundred of its students live in monastic quarters provided or approved by the university, so long must the university be held responsible by the city, by parents, and by society at large, for the sanitary and moral condition of such quarters. The dormitory system implies and necessitates oversight of health and morals. The trouble to-day is that the administrative machinery in use is not capable of doing all that is and ought to be expected of it. . . . If it

be determined openly that the health and morals
of Harvard undergraduates are not to occupy the
attention of the Dean and Board of the college,
then the present system may be perpetuated, but
if this determination is not reached, then either the
system must be changed or the present attempt to
accomplish the impossible will go on until something
snaps."

Since Mr. Bolles's day there has been much earnest effort to solve the administrative problem; but
the difficulties have increased rather than dimin-
ished. The duties of the Dean are still much the
same as when the freshman class numbered one
hundred instead of five. Only the Dean has been
improved. He is at least five times as human and
five times as earnest as any other Dean; but the
freshman class keeps on growing, and when he has
satisfied his very exacting conscience and retires
(or, not having satisfied his conscience, perishes),
no man knows where his better is to be found. Of
the Secretary and the Recorder and his assistants
Mr. Bolles has spoken. A Regent has among
other duties a general charge of the rooms the
fellows live in, and usually makes each room and
its occupant a yearly visit — which the occupant,
in the perversity of undergraduate nature, regards
as a visitation. Then there is the physician. So

large a proportion of the undergraduates were found to be isolated and unhappy in their circumstances, and remote from the knowledge of the authorities, that it became necessary to appoint some one to whom they might appeal in need. Thus the details as to each undergraduate's residence are in the hands of seven different officials, each of whom, in order to attain the best results, requires a personal acquaintance with the thousands of undergraduates. Furthermore the entire body of undergraduates changes every four years. If every administrator had the commodity of lives commonly attributed to the cat, the duties of their offices would still be infinitely beyond them.

Mr. Bolles suggested a solution of the administrative problem : "If the college is too large for its dean and administrative board to manage in the way most certain to benefit its students, it should be divided, using as a divisor the number . . . which experts may agree in thinking is the number of young men whom one dean and board should be expected to know and govern effectively."

When Mr. Bolles wrote, one class of administrative officer and one only was limited in his duties to a single small community : in each building in which students lived, a proctor resided who was supposed to see that the Regent's orders were enforced. Since then another step has been taken in the same direction; a board of advisers has been established, each member of which is supposed to have a helpful care of twenty-five freshmen. These two officials, it will be seen, divide the administrative duties of an English tutor. That they represent a step toward Mr. Bolles's solution of the administrative difficulty has probably never occurred to the authorities; and as yet it must be admitted the step is mainly theoretical. The position of both, as I know from sad personal experience, is such that their duties, like those of all other administrators, resolve into a mere matter of police regulation. The men are apt to resist all friendly advances. In the end, a proctor's activities usually consist in preventing them of a Sunday from shouting too loud over games of indoor football, and at other times from blowing holes through the cornice with shotguns. The case of the freshman adviser is much the same. His first duty is to expound to his charges the mysteries of the elective system, and to help each student choose his courses. According to the original intention, he was to exert as far as possible a beneficial personal influence on newcomers; but the result seldom follows the intention. Beyond the visit which each freshman is obliged to make to his adviser in order to have his list of electives duly signed, there is nothing except misdemeanor to bring the two within the same horizon. When the adviser takes pains to proffer hospitality, the freshman's first thought is that he is to be disciplined. When, as often happens, a proctor is also a freshman adviser, he unites the two administrative duties of an English tutor; but his position is much less favorable in that his duties are performed toward two distinct bodies of men. With time, tact, and labor, he might conceivably force himself into personal relationship with his fifty-odd charges; but the inevitable ground of meeting, such as the English tutor finds in his teaching, is lacking. An attempt to become acquainted is very apt to appear gratuitous. In point of fact, such acquaintance is scarcely expected by the university, and is certainly not paid for. What little an administrator earns is apt to be so much an hour (and not so very much) for teaching. A gratuitous office is so difficult that one hesitates to perform it gratuitously. If the young instructor is bent on making himself unnecessary trouble, there is plenty of opportunity in connection with his teaching; and here, of course, owing to the characteristic lack of organic coördination, he has to deal with a body of men who, except by rare accident, are quite distinct both from those whom he advises and those whom he proctorizes. The system at Harvard may be different in detail from that at other American universities; but wherever a large body of undergraduates are living under a single administrative system, it can scarcely be different in kind.

Enough has been said to show that the only office which an administrator can perform is a police office. Where the college and the university are identical, the element of personal influence is necessarily eliminated. But if the college were divided into separate administrative units, the situation would be very different. The seven general and two special offices I have indicated might be discharged, as regards each undergraduate, by a dean and a few proctor-advisers; and as the students and their officers would be living in the same building, personal knowledge and influence might become the controlling force. The solution of the administrative problem is identical with the solution of the social and athletic problem, and in both cases a movement toward it is begun. If the student body is eventually divided into residential halls of the early mediæval type, much good will result, and probably nothing but good, even if the tutorial function proper is absent. As to the addition of the tutorial function, that is a question of extreme complexity and uncertainty, in order to grasp which it is necessary to review the peculiar educational institutions of American universities.

III

THE EDUCATIONAL PROBLEM

AS regards the American teaching system, the fact that the college so long remained identical with the university has caused little else than good. At Oxford and Cambridge, when a demand arose for instruction in new fields, the university could not meet it because it had little or no wealth and had surrendered its teaching function; and the score of richly endowed colleges, by force of their inertia, collectively resisted the demand. The enlargement in the scope of instruction has been of the slowest. In America, each new demand instantly created its supply. The moment the students in theology required more than a single professor, their tuition fees as well as other funds could be applied to the creation of a divinity school; and the professorships in law, medicine, and the technical professions were likewise organized into schools, each fully equipped under a separate faculty for the pursuit of its special aim. Thus the ancient college was developed by segregation into a fully organized modern university. American institutions are composed of a reduplication, not of similar colleges, but of distinct schools, each with its special subject to teach. This fact makes possible a far higher standard of instruction. The virtue of the administrative and social organization in the English university, as has been pointed out, results from division of the university into separate communities, — distinct organs, each with its separate activity. The virtue of the American university in its teaching functions results from a precisely similar cause.

In the case of the college, one or two details have lately been the occasion of criticism. In the educational as in the social and administrative functions, the machinery is apparently overgrown. Until well into the nineteenth century, the body of instruction offered was much the same as in the English colleges of the seventeenth century, or in the pass schools of to-day, — a modified version of the mediæval trivium and quadrivium. When a new world of intellectual life was opened, most academic leaders regarded it with abhorrence. The old studies were the only studies to develop the manners and the mind; the new studies were barbarous, and dwarfed the understanding. All learning had been contained in a pint-pot, and must continue to be so. If the old curriculum had prevailed, the old system might have continued to serve, in spite of the enormous increase of students; but it did not. Discussions of the educational value of the new learning are still allowed to consume paper and ink; but the cause of the old pint-pot was lost decades ago. All branches are taught, and are open to all students.

The live question to-day both in England and America is not whether we shall recognize the new subjects, but how and in what proportion we shall teach them. In England, where the colleges and the university are separate, the teaching and the examining are separate. The student prepares in college for an examination by the university. It is as a result of this that the subjects of instruction have been divided and organized into honor schools; and here again the division and organization have resulted in sounder and more efficient functioning. In America, such a division has never been made: the teaching and the degree-granting offices have remained identical. The professor in each " course " is also the examiner, and the freedom of choice of necessity goes not by groups of related studies but by small disconnected courses. As the field of recognized knowledge developed, new courses were added, and the student was granted a greater range of choice.

Whereas of old all the instruction of the college might and had to be taken in four years, the modern courses could scarcely be exhausted in a full century. This American system, earliest advocated at Harvard, is called the elective system, and has made its way, in a more or less developed form, into all American universities worthy of the name. Its primary work was that of the Oxford honor schools — the shattering of the old pint-pot. It has done this work; but it is now in train to become no less a superstition than the older system, and is thus no less a menace to the cause of education.

It is perhaps only natural, though it was scarcely to be expected, that the university which in late years has most severely criticised the elective system is that which a quarter of a century ago deliberately advocated it, and in the face of almost universal opposition justified it in the eyes of American educators. There has evidently been a miscalculation. Yet though Harvard has cautiously acknowledged its failure in the persons of no less authorities than Professor Münsterberg and Dean Briggs, the element of error has not yet been clearly stated, nor has the remedy been proposed. Many things have been said against the elective system, but they may all be summed up in one phrase: it is not elective. This is no specious paradox. It is the offer of free election that is specious.

No offer could seem fairer. The student is at liberty to choose as he will. He may specialize microscopically or scatter his attention over the universe; he may elect the most ancient subjects or the most modern, the hardest or the easiest. No offer, I repeat, could seem fairer. But experience disillusions. Some day or other a serious student wakes up to the fact that he is the victim of — shall we say a thimble-rigging game? For example, let us take the case of a serious specialist. Of all the world's knowledge the serious specialist values only one little plot. A multitude of courses is listed in the catalogue, fairly exhausting his field. Delightful! Clearly he can see which walnut-shell covers the pea. He chooses for his first year's study four courses — the very best possible selection, the only selection, to open up his field. One moment: on closer scrutiny he finds that two of the four courses are given at the same hour, and that, therefore, he cannot take them in the same year. Still, there are at his command other courses, not so well adapted to his purposes, but sooner or later necessary. He chooses one. Hold again! On closer inspection he finds that appended to the course is a Roman numeral, and that the same numeral is against one of his other courses. After half an hour's search in the catalogue he finds that, though the two courses are given at different hours, and indeed on different days of the week, the mid-year and final examinations in both take place on the same days. Obviously these two cannot be taken in the same year. With dampened spirits his eye lights on a second substitute. He could easily deny himself this course; but it is vastly interesting, if not important, and he must arrange a year's work. Behold, this most interesting course was given last year, and will be given next year, but neither love nor money nor the void of a soul hungering for knowledge could induce the professor who gives it to deliver one sentence of one lecture; he is busy and more than busy with another course which will not be given next year. The specialist is at last forced to elect a course he does not really want. One entanglement as to hours of which the present deponent had knowledge forced a specialist in Elizabethan literature to elect — and, being a candidate for a degree with distinction, to get a high grade in — a course in the history of finance legislation in the United States. This was a tragic waste, for so many and so minute are the courses offered that the years at the student's disposal are all too few to cover even a comparatively narrow field. The specialist may well ruminate on the philosophy of Alice and her Wonderland jam. Yesterday he could elect anything, and to-morrow anything; but how empty is to-day!

Highly as the modern university · regards the serious specialist, a more general sympathy will probably be given to the man who is seeking a liberal education. Such a man knows that in four years at his disposal he cannot gain any real scientific knowledge even of the studies of the old-fashioned college curriculum. As taught now, at Harvard, they would occupy, according to President Eliot's report for 1894–95, twice four years. But by choosing a single group of closely related subjects, and taking honors in it, he hopes to master a considerable plot of the field of knowledge. I will not say that he chooses the ancient classics, for — though they are admirably taught in a general way in the great Oxford Honor School of Literæ Humaniores — the American student may be held to require, even in studying the classics, a larger element of scientific culture, which would take more time than is to be had. For the same reason I will not say that he chooses the modern languages and literatures, though such a choice might be defended. Let us say that he chooses a

single modern language and literature — his own.[1]
Surely this is not too large a field for four years'
study. Of classics, mathematics, science, and history he has supposedly been given a working
knowledge in the preparatory school. For the rest
he relies on the elective system.

Even in the beginning, like the specialist, he is
unable to choose the courses he most wants, because of the conflict of the hours of instruction and
examination; and this difficulty pursues him year
by year, increasing as the subjects to be taken
grow fewer and fewer. But let us dismiss this as
an incidental annoyance. His fate is foreshadowed
when he finds that the multitude of courses by
which alone he could cover the entire field of English literature would fill twice the time at his disposal. Already he has discovered that the elective
system is not so very elective. He sadly omits
Icelandic and Gothic, and all but one half course
is Anglo-Saxon. Some day he means to cover the
ground by means of a history of literature and
translations; but in point of fact, as the subjects
are not at all necessary for his degree, and as he
is overburdened with other work, he never does.

---

[1] For a detailed statement as to the course such a student would
be able to pursue under the English system of honor schools, see
Appendix III.

He sticks to his last, and is the more willing to do so because, being wise beyond the wont of undergraduates, he knows that it will be well to fortify his knowledge of the English language and literature with a complementary knowledge of the history of the English people, and of the history and literature of the neighboring Germans and French.

Having barely time for a rapid survey of these complementary subjects, he elects only the introductory courses. In the aggregate they require many precious hours, and to take them he is obliged to omit outright English literature of the eighteenth and nineteenth centuries; but he knows that it is better to neglect a finial or two than the buttresses of the edifice he is building. Again he has miscalculated. After his complementary courses are begun, and it is too late to withdraw from them, he discovers even more clearly than the specialist how very unelective the elective system can be. It is the same old question of the thimble and the pea. These introductory courses are intended to introduce him to the study of history and of literature, not to complement his studies of English. What he wanted to know in English history was the social and the political movements, the vital and picturesque aspect; what he is taught is the sources and constitutions — the dry bones.

In German and French he wanted to know the epochs of literature; he is taught the language, considered scientifically, or, at most, certain haphazard authors in whom he has only a casual interest. If he is studying for honors, he is obliged to waste enough time on these disappointing courses to reach a high grade in each. The system of free election is mighty, for he is a slave to it.

This difficulty is typical. Thus a student of history or of German who wants to study Elizabethan literature for its bearing on his subject is obliged to spend one full course — a quarter of a year's work — on the language of four or five plays of Shakespeare before he is permitted to take a half course on Shakespeare as a dramatist; and even then all the rest of the Elizabethan period is untouched.

Let us suppose that our student of English is wary as well as wise, preternaturally wary, and leaves all complementary subjects to private reading — for which he has no time. He is then able to devote himself to the three or four most important epochs in English literature. He has to leave out much that is of importance, so that he cannot hope to gain a synoptic view of the field as a whole; but of his few subjects he will at least be master. Here at last is the thimble that covers the pea. Not yet! In four courses out of five of those devoted to the greatest writers, the teacher's attention is directed primarily to a very special and scientific study of the language; the examination consists in explaining linguistic cruxes. Literary criticism, even of the most sober kind, is quite neglected. If the student learns only what is taught, he may attain the highest grades and the highest honors without being able in the end to distinguish accurately the spirit of Chaucer from that of Elizabethan literature.

Furthermore, not every student is sufficiently well advised to know precisely what courses he requires to attain his end. For example, to gain an understanding of the verse forms and even the spirit of Middle English and Elizabethan English, it is necessary to know the older French and Italian; but, as it happened, our student was not aware of the fact until he broke his shins against it, and it was nobody's business to tell him of it. And even if he had been aware of it, he could not have taken those subjects without leaving great gaps in his English studies. He has graduated *summa cum laude* and with highest honors in English; but he has not even a correct outline knowledge of his subject. His education is a thing of shreds and patches.

Whatever may be the aim of the serious student, the elective system is similarly fatal to it. I must be content with a single instance more. The signal merit of the old-fashioned curriculum was that its insistence on the classics and mathematics insured a mental culture and discipline of a very high order, and of a kind that is impossible where the student elects only purely scientific courses, or courses in which he happens to be especially interested. Let us suppose that the serious student wishes to elect his courses so as to receive this discipline. His plight is indicated in "Some Old-fashioned Doubts about New-fashioned Education" which have lately been divulged[1] by the Dean of Harvard College, Professor Le B. R. Briggs. The undergraduate "may choose the old studies but not the old instruction. Instruction under an elective system is aimed at the specialist. In elective mathematics, for example, the non-mathematical student who takes the study for self-discipline finds the instruction too high for him; indeed, he finds no encouragement for electing mathematics at all." The same is true of the classics.

One kind of student, to be quite candid, profits vastly by the elective system, namely, the student whose artistic instinct makes him ambitious of

---

[1] *The Atlantic Monthly*, October, 1900.

gaining the maximum effect, an A. B., with the minimum expenditure of means. History D is a good course : the lectures do not come until eleven o'clock, and no thought of them blunts the edge of the evening before. Semitic C is another good course — only two lectures a week, and you can pass it with a few evenings of cramming. If such a man is fortunate enough to have learned foreign languages in the nursery or in traveling abroad, he elects all the general courses in French and German. This sort of man is regarded by Dean Briggs with unwonted impatience ; but he has one great claim to our admiration. Of all possible kinds of students, he alone has found the pea. For him the elective system is elective.

The men who developed the elective system, it is quite unnecessary to say, had no sinister intention. They were pioneers of educational progress who revolted against the narrowness of the old curriculum. The nearest means of reform was suggested to them by the German plan, and they sought to naturalize this *in toto* without regard to native needs and conditions. But the pioneer work of the elective system has been done, and the men who now uphold it in its entirety are clogging the wheels of progress no less than those who fought it at the outset. The logic of circumstances early forced them

to the theory that all knowledge is of equal importance, provided only that it is scientifically pursued,
and this position in effect they still maintain.
You may elect to study Shakespeare and end by
studying American finance legislation ; but so long
as you are compelled to study scientifically, bless
you, you are free.

The serenity of these men must of late have been
somewhat clouded. Professor Hugo Münsterberg,
as an editorial writer in " Scribner's Magazine "
lately remarked, " has been explaining, gently but
firmly, ostensibly to the teachers in secondary
schools, but really to his colleagues in the Harvard
faculty, that they are not imitating the German
method successfully." In no way is the American
college man in the same case as the German undergraduate. His preparatory schooling is likely to
be three years in arrears, and, in any case, what he
seeks is usually culture, not science. " The new
notion of scholarship," this writer continues, " by
which the degree means so much Latin and Greek,
or the equivalent of them in botany or blacksmith-
ing, finds no favor at all in what is supposed to
be the native soil of the ' elective system.' " Dr.
Münsterberg's own words, guarded as they are, are
not without point : " Even in the college two thirds
of the elections are haphazard, controlled by acci-

dental motives; election, of course, demands a wide view and broad knowledge of the whole field. . . . A helter-skelter chase of the unknown is no election." The writer in "Scribner's" concludes: "It is not desirable that a man should sell his birthright for a mess of pottage, even if he gets the pottage. If he does not get it, as Dr. Münsterberg intimates, of course his state is even worse."

Rough as the elective system is upon the student who aspires to be merely a scholar, it is rougher on the undergraduate who only wants to train his mind and to equip it for business and professional life. To him a purely scientific training is usually a positive detriment. Scrupulous exactitude and a sense of the elusiveness of all knowledge are an excellent and indispensable part of the bringing up of a scholar; but few things are more fitted, if pursued exclusively, to check the self-confidence of a normal man and to blight his will. Poor Richard had a formula for the case: "A handsaw is a very good thing, but not to shave with." Before taking a vigorous hold on the affairs of Wall Street or of Washington, our recent graduate has first to get away from most of the standards that obtain in the university, or at least to supplement them by a host of others which he should have learned there. In another passage in the article already quoted,

Dean Briggs has touched the vital spot. He is speaking of the value, to teachers especially, of the peculiar fetich of Teutonized university instruction, the thesis, and of its liability to be of fictitious value. " Such theses, I suspect, have more than once been accepted for higher degrees; yet higher degrees won through them leave the winner farther from the best qualities of a teacher, remote from men and still more remote from boys. It was a relief the other day to hear a head-master say, ' I am looking for an under-teacher. I want first a man, and next a man to teach.' " What is true of teaching is even more obviously true of the great world of business and of politics. What it wants is men.

The cause of the break-down of the elective system, as at present constituted, is to be found in the machinery of instruction. The office of the teacher has become inextricably mixed up with a totally alien office — university discipline. Attendance at lectures is the only means of recording a student's presence in the university, and success in the examination in lecture courses is the only basis for judging of his diligence. At the tolling of a bell the student leaves all other affairs to report at a certain place. In the Middle Ages, as we have seen, lectures were of necessity the main means of instruction. Books were rare and their prices prohibitive.

The master read and the student copied. To-day, there are tens of thousands of books in every college library. Only in the higher courses are lectures necessary or profitable. But still instruction is carried on, even in the most general courses, by means of professorial lectures. Where great periods are covered by leaps and bounds, freshness or individuality of treatment is quite impossible. The tolling of the college bell dooms hundreds of students to hear a necessarily hurried and inarticulate statement of knowledge which has been carefully handled in printed form by the most brilliant writers, and to which a tutor might refer the student in a few minutes' conference. Modify the lecture system? It is the foundation of the police regulation. The boasted freedom in elective studies simmers down to this, that it enables the student to choose in what courses he shall be made the unwilling ally of the administrative officer. The lectures waste the time of the student and exhaust the energy of the teacher; but unless the lecturers give them and the studious attend, how can the university know that the shiftless stay away?

It is necessary, moreover, for the administrator to judge of the student's success as well as of his diligence. Twice every year the professors hold an examination lasting for three hours in each of their several courses. Of late years an ingenious means has been devised for making the examination system an even more perfect ally of the police. In the middle of each term an examination of one hour is held to insure that the student has not only attended lectures but studied outside; and, in order to expose the procrastinator, it has become the custom for the examination to be given without warning. Like the lecture system, the examination system throws the onus of discipline on the studious and the teachers. Two thousand students write yearly 32,000 examination books. Quite obviously the most advanced of the professors cannot spare time for the herculean task of reading and duly grading their share of these books. They give over most of them to underpaid assistants. The logical result of such a system is that the examinations tend to be regarded merely as statements of fact, and the reading of the books merely as clerical labor. If academic distinctions are disprized in America, both in college and out of it, this is amply explained by the fact that they attest a student's diligence rather than his ability. They are awarded, like a Sunday-school prize, in return for a certain number of good-conduct checks.

It is not enough that the machinery of instruction wastes the time of the student and debases the office of the examiner; it is, as I have said, the cause of the break-down of the elective system. As long as each student is required to pursue every study under the eye of the disciplinarian, the decision as to what he shall study rests not with his desires or his needs, but with an elaborate schedule of lectures and examinations. So excessive are the evils of the present system that no less a man than Professor William James has advocated the abolition of the examinations.

This remedy is perhaps extreme; but the only alternative is almost as radical. It is to enable the student, at least the more serious student, to slip the trammels of the elective system, and to study rationally, and to be rationally examined in, the subject or group of subjects which he prefers. In a word, the remedy is to divide and organize our courses of instruction for the more serious students into groups corresponding in some measure to what the English·call honor schools.

It may be objected that already it is possible to read for honors. The objection will scarcely convince any one who has taken the examination. It is oral, and occupies an hour ˙or two. The men who conduct it are leading men in the department, and are often of world-wide reputation. They are so great that they understand the nature of the farce they are playing. No candidate is expected to have covered the field of his honor subject even in the broadest outlines. When the astute student is not sure of an answer, he candidly admits the fact and receives credit for knowing that he does not know — a cardinal virtue to the scientific mind. If I may be allowed a personal instance, I went up for the examination in English literature in complete ignorance as to all but a single brief movement. When my ignorances were laid bare, the examiners most considerately confined their questions to my period. We had much pleasant conversation. Each of the examiners had imparted in his courses his latest rays of new light, and each in turn gave me the privilege of reflecting these rays to the others. For a brief but happy hour my importance was no less than that of the most eminent publication of the learned world. It need scarcely be said that such examinations are not supposed to have much weight in judging of the candidate's fitness. A more important test is a thesis studied from original sources, and the most important is good-conduct marks in a certain arbitrary number of set lecture courses. The policeman's examination is supreme.

IV

THE AMERICAN HALL

THE college has shown a tendency, as I have indicated, to divide in its social life into separate organizations for the purposes of residence, dining, and athletics. In the administrative life, at least the proctors and the freshman advisers are each in charge of separate bodies of undergraduates. In the educational life, a similar tendency is noticeable. Year by year there has been an increasing disposition to supplement lectures or to substitute them by what is in effect tutorial instruction. In the history courses, for example, the lectures and examinations have for some time been supplemented by private personal conferences. If the student is proceeding properly, he is encouraged; if not, he is given the necessary guidance and assistance. I do not know what the result has been in the teaching of history; but in the teaching of English composition, where the conferences have largely supplanted lectures, it has been an almost unmixed benefit. The instructor's comments are given a directness and a personal interest impossible either in the lecture-room or by means of written correction and criticism; and the students are usually eager to discuss their work and the means for bettering it. As the lecture system proves more and more inadequate, the tutorial instruction must necessarily continue to increase, and is not unlikely to afford the basis for a more sensibly devised scheme of honor schools.

If the American college were organized into separate halls, it would be necessary and proper, as Mr. Bolles suggested, to place in each a Dean and administrative board; and the most economical plan of administration, as he pointed out, would be to give each administrator as many duties as possible toward a single set of pupils. Thus the proctor on each staircase of the hall would be the adviser of the men who roomed on it. It would be only a logical extension of the principle to give the proctor-adviser a tutorial office. All this indicates a reversion toward the golden age of the mediæval hall.

Here is where the gain would lie: The administration of the hall would make it no longer necessary to rely on the lecture courses for police duty, and the wise guidance of a tutor would in some measure remove the necessity of the recurrent police examinations. Thus the student would be able to elect such courses only as the competent adviser might judge best for him; and if the faculty were relieved of the labor of unnecessary instruction and examination it would be possible, with less expense than the present system involves, to offer a well-considered honor examination, and to provide that the examination books should be graded not with mere clerical intelligence, but with the highest available critical appreciation. Thus and only thus can the American honor degree be given that value as an asset which the English honor degree has possessed for almost a century.

It would by no means be necessary as at Oxford to make the honor examination the only basis for granting the degree. The fewer lecture courses which the student found available would be those in which the instruction is more advanced — the " university " courses properly speaking; and his examinations in these would be a criterion, such as Oxford is very much in need of, for correcting the evidence of the honor examination. Furthermore, in connection with one or more of these courses it would be easy for the student to prepare an honor thesis studied from the original sources under the constant advice of a university professor. Such an arrangement might be made to combine in any desired proportion the merits of the English honor schools with the merits of advanced instruction in America. With the introduction of the tutor, the American hall would be the complete counterpart of the mediæval hall of the golden age, and would solve the educational as well as the social and administrative problem.

As to the details of the new system, experience would be the final teacher; but for a first experiment, the English arrangement is in its main outline suggestive. An American pass degree might be taken by electing, as all students now elect, a certain number of courses at random. For the increasing number of those who can afford only three years' study, a pass degree would probably prove of the greatest advantage. It was by making this sharp distinction between the pass degree and the honor degree that the English universities long ago solved the question, much agitated still in America, of the three years' course. For the honor men [1] two general examinations would probably suffice. For his second year honor examination (the English " Moderations ") a student might select from three or four general groups. This examination would necessarily offer precisely

[1] For full details as to the scheme of an English honor school, see Appendix III.

that opportunity for mental culture the lack of which Dean Briggs laments as the worst feature of the elective system as at present conducted. Furthermore, it would be easy to arrange the second year honor groups so as to include only such subjects as are serviceable both for the purposes of a general education and to lead up to the subjects the student is likely to elect for final honors. For the final honor examination the student might choose from a dozen or more honor groups, in any one of which he would receive scientific culture of the most advanced type, while at the same time, by means of private reading under his tutor, he might fill in very pleasantly the outlines of his subject. It is probable that such a system would even facilitate the efforts of those who are endeavoring to transplant German standards. According to Professor Münsterberg, the student who specializes in the German university is a good two years or more in advance of the American freshman. The spirit of German instruction would thus require that the period of general culture be extended at least to the middle of the undergraduate course.

Some such reorganization of our methods of teaching and examining, and I fear only this, would enable an undergraduate to choose what he wants and to pursue it with a fair chance of success. It would make the elective system elective.

A concrete plan for an American hall will perhaps make the project clearer. The poorer students at Harvard have for some years had a separate dining-hall, Foxcroft, where the fare and the system of paying for it are adapted to the slenderest of purses. They have also lived mainly in certain primitive dormitories in which the rooms are cheapest. More than any other set of men except the clubmen they are a united body, or are capable of being made so. When next a bequest is received, might not the University erect a building in which a hundred or two of these men could live in common? The quadrangle would insure privacy, the first requisite of community life; the kitchen and dining-hall would insure the maximum comfort and convenience with the minimum expense. Nothing could contribute more to the self-respect and the general standing of the poorer students than a comfortable and well-ordered place and way of living, if only because nothing could more surely correct the idiosyncrasies in manners and appearance which are fostered by their present discomfort and isolation.

The life of the hall would not of course be as strictly regulated as the life in an English college

—perhaps no more strictly than in any other American college building. If in the hope of creating a closer community feeling stricter rules were adopted, they should be adopted, as in a mediæval hall, only by consent of the undergraduates.

Such a hall would develop athletic teams of its own, and would produce university athletes. Under the present arrangement, when the poorer students are members of university teams, they may, and often do, become honorary members of the university clubs ; but their lack of means and sometimes of the manner of the world make it difficult for them to be at home in the clubs; their social life is usually limited to a small circle of friends. If they had first been trained in the life of a hall, they would more easily fall in with the broader life outside ; and instead of being isolated as at present, they would exert no small influence both in their hall and in the university. Few things could be better for the general life of the undergraduate than the coöperation of such men, and few things could be better for the members of a hall than to be brought by means of its leading members into close connection with the life of the university.

If such a hall were successful, it could not fail to attract serious students of all sorts and conditions. At Oxford, Balliol has for generations been

known as in the main unfashionable and scholarly ;
but it is seldom without a blue or two, and its eight
has often been at the head of the river. As a result of all this, it never ceases to attract the more
serious men from the aristocracy and even the nobility. In America, the success of one residential
hall would probably lead to the establishment of
others, so that in the end the life of the university
might be given all the advantages of a dual organization.

No change could be more far reaching and beneficial. The American institutions of the present
are usually divided into two classes, the university,
or "large college," and the " small college." The
merit of the large colleges is that those fortunately placed in them gain greater familiarity with
the ways of the world and of men, while for those
who wish it, they offer more advanced instruction
— the instruction characteristic of German universities. But to the increasing number of undergrad-
nates who are not fortunately placed, their very size
is the source of unhappiness; and for those undergraduates who wish anything else than scientific instruction, their virtues become merely a detriment.
It is for this reason that many wise parents still
prefer to intrust the education of their sons to the
small colleges. These small colleges possess many

of the virtues of the English universities; they train the mind and cultivate it, and at the same time develop the social man. If now the American university were to divide its undergraduate department into organized residential halls, it would combine the advantages of the two types of American institution, which are the two types of instruction the world over. Already our college life at its best is as happy as the college life in England; and the educational advantages of the four or five of our leading universities are rapidly becoming equal to those of the four or five leading universities in Germany. A combination of the residential hall and the teaching university would reproduce the highest type of the university of the Middle Ages; and in proportion as life and knowledge have been bettered in six hundred years, it would better that type. England has lost the educational virtues of the mediæval university, while Germany, in losing the residential halls, has lost its peculiar social virtues. When the American university combines the old social life with the new instruction, it will be the most perfect educational instruction in the history of civilization.

APPENDIX

APPENDIX

I. ATHLETIC TRAINING IN ENGLAND

IN one or two particulars it seemed to me that we might learn from the English methods of training. On the Oxford team we took long walks every other day instead of track work. Our instructions were to climb all the hills in our way. This was in order to bring into play new muscles as far as possible, so as to rest those used in running. Though similar walks are sometimes given in America as a preliminary " seasoning," our training, for months before a meeting, is confined to the track. This is not unwise as long as a runner's stride needs developing; and in the heat of our summers such walks as the English take might sometimes prove exhausting. Yet my personal observations convinced me that for distance runners — and for sprinters, too, perhaps — the English method is far better. Under our training the muscles often seem overpowered by nervous lassitude ; at the start of a race I have often felt it an effort to stand. In England there was little or none of this; we felt, as the bottle-holders are fond of putting it, " like a magnum of champagne."

This idea of long walks, which the English have arrived at empirically, has been curiously approved in

America by scientific discovery. It has been shown
that after muscles appear too stiff from exhaustion to
move, they can be excited to action by electric currents; while the motor nerves on being examined after
such fatigue are found to be shrunken and empty, as in
extreme old age. The limit of muscular exertion is thus
clearly determined by the limit of the energy of the motor
nerve. Now in a perfectly trained runner, the heart and
lung must obviously reach their prime simultaneously
with the motor nerves used in running; but since these
organs are ordained to supply the entire system with fuel,
they will usually require a longer time to reach prime
condition than any single set of nerves. Thus continual
track work is likely to develop the running nerves to the
utmost before the heart and lungs are at prime. Con-
versely stated, if the development of the running nerves
is retarded so as to keep pace with the development of
the heart and lungs, the total result is likely to be higher.
All this amounts to what any good English trainer will
tell you — that you must take long walks on up and down
grades in order to rest your running muscles and at the
same time give your heart and lungs plenty of work —
that is, in order to keep from getting "track stale."

The amount of work we did from day to day will best
be understood, perhaps, by quoting one or two of the
training-cards. For the hundred yards the training
during the final ten days was as follows: *Monday* and
Tuesday, sprints (three or four dashes of sixty yards at
top speed); *Wednesday*, a fast 120 yards at the Queen's

Club grounds; *Thursday*, walk; *Friday*, sprints; *Saturday*, 100 yards trial at Queen's Club; *Sunday*, walk; *Monday*, light work at Queen's Club; *Tuesday*, easy walk; *Wednesday*, inter-varsity sports. The man for whom this card was written happened to be over weight and short of training, or he would have had less track work. If he had been training for the quarter in addition to the hundred, he would have had fewer sprints, and, instead of the fast 120, a trial quarter a week before the sports, with perhaps a fast 200 on the following Friday. For the mile, the following is a characteristic week's work, ending with a trial: *Sunday*, walk; *Monday*, one lap ($\frac{1}{3}$ mile); *Tuesday*, two laps, fastish; *Wednesday*, walk; *Thursday*, easy mile; *Friday*, walk; *Saturday*, a two lap trial (at the rate of 4.30 for the mile). For the three miles, the following is a schedule of the first ten days (the walks are unusually frequent because the " first string " had a bruise on the ball of his foot): *Monday*, walk; *Tuesday*, walk; *Wednesday*, two slow laps at the Queen's Club; *Thursday*, walk; *Friday*, walk; *Saturday*, a long run at the Queen's Club; *Sunday*, walk; *Monday*, four laps, fastish, at the Queen's Club; *Tuesday*, walk; *Wednesday*, inter-varsity sports. The chief difference between this work and what we should give in America is in the matter of walking.

APPENDIX

II. CLIMATE AND INTERNATIONAL ATHLETICS

THE value of international contests as a basis for comparing English and American training is impaired by the fact that the visiting team is pretty sure to be under the weather, as may be indicated by summarizing the history of international contests. The first representatives we sent abroad, the Harvard four-oared crew of 1869, became so overtrained on the Thames on work which would have been only sufficient at home, that two of the four men had to be substituted. The substitutes were taken from the "second" crew, which had just come over from the race at Worcester. The men in this crew had been so inferior as oarsmen that they had been allowed to compete against Yale only after vigorous protest; but in the race against Oxford, owing probably to the brevity of their training in England, the substitutes pulled the strongest oars in the boat. The crew got off very well, but when the time came for the final effort, the two original members had not the nervous stamina to respond.

The experience of the Yale athletes who competed against Oxford in 1894 was much the same. Their performances in the games were so far below their American form that they won only the events in which they literally outclassed their opponents — the hammer, shot, and broad jump. They were sportsmen enough not to explain their poor showing, and perhaps they never quite realized how the soft and genial English summer had unnerved them; but several competent observers who had watched their practice told me that they lost form from day to day. Their downfall was doubtless aided by the fact that instead of training at Brighton or elsewhere on the coast, they trained in the Thames valley and at Oxford.

The experience of the Cornell crew, of which I got full and frank information while crossing the Atlantic with them after the race, was along the same lines. Before leaving Ithaca, they rowed over the equivalent of the Henley course in time that was well under seven minutes, and not far from the Henley record of six minutes, fifty-one seconds. At Henley they rowed their first trial in seven minutes and three seconds, if my memory serves, and in consequence were generally expected to win. From that day they grew worse and worse. Certain of the eight went stale and had to be substituted. In the race the crew, like the earlier Harvard crew, went to pieces when they were called on for a spurt — the test of nerve force in reserve — and were beaten in wretchedly slow time. They had gone hopelessly stale on work which would have been none too much in America.

The experience of the Yale crew in the year after was similar to that of Harvard and Cornell. The crew went to pieces and lost the race for the lack of precisely that burst of energy for which American athletes, and Yale in particular, are remarkable.

Meantime one or two American athletes training at Oxford had been gathering experience, which, humble though it was, had the merit of being thorough. Mr. J. L. Bremer, who will be remembered in America as making a new world's record over the low hurdles, steadily lost suppleness and energy at Oxford, so that he was beaten in the quarter mile in time distinctly inferior to his best in America. Clearly, the effect of the English climate is to relax the nervous system and thereby to reduce the athlete's power both of sprinting *per se* and of spurting at the finish of the race. My own experience in English training confirmed the conclusion, and pointed to an interesting extension of it. I was forced to conclude that the first few weeks in England are more than likely to undo an athlete, and especially for sprinting; and even if he stays long enough to find himself again, his ability to sprint is likely to be lessened. In the long run, on the other hand, the English climate produces staying power in almost the same proportion as it destroys speed.

When the joint team of track athletes from Yale and Harvard went to England in 1899, the powers that were took advantage of past experiences, and instead of going to the Thames valley to train, they went to Brighton; and instead of doing most of their training in England, they gave themselves only the few days necessary to get their shore legs and become acquainted with the Queen's Club track. As a result, the team was in general up to its normal form, or above it, and, except for the fact that one of the men was ill, would have won.

The experience of the English athletes who came to

America in 1895 points to a similar conclusion. Though the heat was intense and oppressive and most of the visitors were positively sick, one of the sprinters, in spite of severe illness, was far above his previous best, while all of the distance men went quite to pieces. Thus our climate would seem to reduce the staying power of the English athletes, and perhaps to increase the speed of sprinters.

It appears on the whole probable that in these international contests the visiting athlete had best do as much as possible of his training at home, and it follows that the visiting team is at a distinct and inevitable disadvantage.

III. AN OXFORD FINAL HONOR SCHOOL

THE scope and content of an English honor school is well illustrated in the following passage from the Oxford examination statutes, which treats of the final school in English literature. The system will be seen to be very different from a system under which a student may receive honors in ignorance of all but a single movement in English literature.

§ 10. *Of the Honour School of English Language and Literature.*

1. The Examination in the School of English Language and Literature shall always include authors or portions of authors belonging to the different periods of

English literature, together with the history of the English language and the history of English literature.

The Examination shall also include Special Subjects falling within or usually studied in connexion with the English language and literature.

2. Every Candidate shall be expected to have studied the authors or portions of authors which he offers (1) with reference to the forms of the language, (2) as examples of literature, and (3) in their relation to the history and thought of the period to which they belong.

He shall also be expected to show a competent knowledge (1) of the chief periods of the English language, including Old English (Anglo-Saxon), and (2) of the relation of English to the languages with which it is etymologically connected, and (3) of the history of English literature, and (4) of the history, especially the social history, of England during the period of English literature which he offers.

3. The Examination in Special Subjects may be omitted by Candidates who do not aim at a place in the First or Second Class.

4. No Candidate shall be admitted to examination in the Final Honour School of English Language and Literature, unless he has either obtained Honours in some Final Honour School or has passed the First Public Examination [*i. e.* Moderation].

5. The Examination shall be under the supervision of a Board of Studies.

6. It shall be the duty of the Board of Studies in framing regulations, and also of the Examiners in the conduct of the Examination, to see that as far as possible equal weight is given to language and literature: provided always that Candidates who offer Special Subjects shall be at liberty to choose subjects connected either with language or with literature or with both.

7. The Board of Studies shall by notice from time to time make regulations respecting the Examination; and shall have power —

(1) To prescribe authors or portions of authors.

(2) To specify one or more related languages or dialects to be offered either as a necessary or as an optional part of the Examination.

(3) To name periods of the history of English literature, and to fix their limits.

(4) To issue lists of Special Subjects in connexion either with language or with literature or with both, prescribing books or authorities where they think it desirable.

(5) To prescribe or recommend authors or portions of authors in languages other than English, to be studied in connexion with Special Subjects to which they are intimately related.

(6) To determine whether Candidates who aim at a place in the First or Second Class shall be required to offer more than one Special Subject.

APPENDIX

The subjects of examination in this School are —

    I. Portions of English Authors.

    II. The History of the English Language.

    III. The History of English Literature.

    IV. (In the case of those Candidates who aim at a place in the First or Second Class) a Special Subject of Language or Literature.

I. ENGLISH AUTHORS.

Candidates will be examined in the following texts :—

Beowulf.

The texts printed in Sweet's *Anglo-Saxon Reader.*

King Horn.

Havelok.

Laurence Minot.

Sir Gawain and the Green Knight.

Chaucer's *Canterbury Tales,* the *Prologue* and the following Tales : —

> *The Knight's, The Man of Law's, The Prioress's, Sir Thopas, The Monk's, The Nun's Priest's, The Pardoner's, The Clerk's, The Squire's, The Second Nun's, The Canon's Yeoman's.*

> *Piers Plowman,* the *Prologue* and first seven *passus* (text B).

> Shakespeare, with a special study of the following Plays : *Midsummer Night's Dream, King John,*

322

Much Ado about Nothing, Macbeth, Cymbe-line.

Milton, with a special study of *Paradise Lost.*

These texts are to be studied (1) with reference to the forms of the language ; (2) as examples of literature ; and (3) in their relation to the history and thought of the period to which they belong.

After Milton no special texts are prescribed, but Candidates are expected to show an adequate knowledge of the chief authors.

II. HISTORY OF THE ENGLISH LANGUAGE.

Candidates will be examined in the Philology and History of the Language, in Gothic (the Gospel of St. Mark), and in Translation from Old English and Middle English authors not specially offered.

III. HISTORY OF ENGLISH LITERATURE.

The Examination in the History of English Literature will not be limited to the prescribed texts. It will include the history of criticism and of style in prose and verse ; for these subjects, Candidates are recommended to consult the following works : —

Sidney, *Apology for Poetry.*

Daniel, *Defence of Rhyme.*

Dryden, *Essay of Dramatic Poesy,* and *Preface to Fables.*

Addison, Papers on Milton in the *Spectator.*

Pope, *Essay on Criticism.*

APPENDIX

Johnson, *Preface to Shakespeare* and *Lives of the Poets.*

Wordsworth, *Prefaces, etc., to Lyrical Ballads.*

Coleridge, *Biographia Literaria.*

IV. SPECIAL SUBJECTS.

Candidates who aim at a place in the First or Second Class will be expected to offer a Special Subject, which may be chosen from the following list: —

1. Old English Language and Literature to 1150 A. D.

2. Middle English Language and Literature, 1150–1400 A. D.

3. Old French Philology, with special reference to Anglo-Norman French, together with a special study of the following texts: —

> Computus of Philippe de Thaun, Voyage of St. Brandan, The Song of Dermot and the Earl, Les contes moralisés de Nicole Bozon.

4. Scandinavian Philology, with special reference to Icelandic, together with a special study of the following texts: —

> Gylfaginning, Laxdæla Saga, Gunnlaugssaga Ormstungu.

5. Elizabethan literature, 1558–1637 A. D.

6. English literature, 1637–1700 A. D.

7. English literature, 1700–1745 A. D.

8. Wordsworth and his contemporaries, 1797–1850 A. D.

9. History of Scottish poetry to 1600 A. D.

APPENDIX

Candidates who desire to offer any other subject or period as a Special Subject must obtain the leave of the Board of Studies a year before the Examination.

Candidates who offer a period of English Literature will be expected to show a competent knowledge of the History, especially the Social History, of England during such period.

The following scheme of papers is contemplated: —

1. Beowulf and other Old English texts.
2. King Horn, Havelok, Minot, Sir Gawain.
3. Chaucer and Piers Plowman.
4. Shakespeare.
5. Milton.
6. History of the language.
7. Gothic — O. E. and M. E. translations.
8. ⎱ History of the Literature, including questions
9. ⎰   on the history of criticism. Two papers, (1) to 1700, (2) after 1700.
10. Special Subjects.